THE TITANIC FLEET
THE SHIPS INVOLVED IN THE TITANIC DISASTER

RICHARD M. JONES

This book is dedicated to all those who lost their lives on the ships involved in the Titanic *story*

You are remembered

First published 2025

Amberley Publishing
The Hill, Stroud,
Gloucestershire, GL5 4EP

www.amberley-books.com

Copyright © Richard M. Jones, 2025

The right of Richard M. Jones to be identified as the Author of this work has been asserted in accordance with the Copyright, Designs and Patents Act 1988.

All rights reserved. No part of this book may be reprinted or reproduced or utilised in any form or by any electronic, mechanical or other means, now known or hereafter invented, including photocopying and recording, or in any information storage or retrieval system, without the permission in writing from the Publishers.

ISBN: 978 1 3981 2603 9 (print)
ISBN: 978 1 3981 2604 6 (ebook)

British Library Cataloguing in Publication Data.
A catalogue record for this book is available from the British Library.

Typeset in 10pt on 13pt Celeste.
Typesetting by SJmagic DESIGN SERVICES, India.
Printed in the UK.

Appointed GPSR EU Representative: Easy Access System Europe Oü, 16879218
Address: Mustamäe tee 50, 10621, Tallinn, Estonia
Contact Details: gpsr.requests@easproject.com, +358 40 500 3575

Contents

Introduction 4

1. Titanic 6
2. Olympic 11
3. Britannic 15
4. Carpathia 19
5. Californian 23
6. Mesaba 26
7. Rappahannock 29
8. Baltic 31
9. New York 35
10. Mackay-Bennett 38
11. Minia 41
12. Montmagny 43
13. Algerine 45
14. Mount Temple 47
15. La Touraine 51
16. Lapland 53
17. Nomadic 57
18. Traffic 61
19. Caronia 63
20. Noordam 68
21. Samson 71
22. Amerika 73
23. Prinz Adalbert 78
24. Niagara 80
25. Frankfurt 82
26. Virginian 84
27. Birma 87
28. Parisian 89
29. Antillian 91
30. Asian 93

Bibliography and Sources 95
Acknowledgements 96

Introduction

In November 1991, when I was still just a child, *Titanic* fever gripped me. I sat down to watch the film *Raise the Titanic*, a fictional action/adventure story based on the book by Clive Cussler, and that day a spark was lit that was to change my life and is still having an effect on me today. Now, over three decades on, several things are remarkably clear: the story of the *Titanic* is well known and popular, and, with the thousands of books written about this doomed ship, you can research almost everything there is to know about it. However, one thing that struck me more than any other was how so many books told the same story, in some cases repeating the same mistakes even down to identical spelling errors. The question I had to ask was what more was there to talk about regarding a ship that only actually sailed for just four days?

That the loss of the *Titanic* is a fascinating story is undisputed, but the discovery of the wreck in 1985 and the release of the films *A Night to Remember* in 1958 and James Cameron's big-budget blockbuster *Titanic* in 1997 spawned further interest. This has continued into the twenty-first century and was particularly high around the time of the centenary commemorations that took place on the anniversary in 2012.

As a consequence, every part of the story seems to have been covered time and time again, with so many people concentrating on the building, the sailing, the people, the wreck, the crew, and even studying certain compartments on board. What new information could be brought to the table?

It dawned on me that nobody had ever written about the other ships involved in the story. Considering the *Titanic* was only around for a short period of time, it is incredible just how many other vessels played a key role in the life of the ship and the people on board. These ships were not without controversy, many of them having had a fascinating career, serving their owners, their country and even taking on important historical roles such as the Dunkirk evacuation of 1940 and rescuing injured troops in the Aegean Sea during the First World War. Each ship had its own story, and some are just as fascinating as that of the *Titanic*, but many are simply forgotten, their only mention in the history books highlighting their role at the time of the 1912 disaster.

Over the years some of these ships have come to light in documentaries, as in the case of the *Mackay-Bennett* and *Britannic*. Some have had their wrecks located on the seabed, such as the *Carpathia* and *Mesaba*, and others, such as the *Californian*, continue to be the focus of an inquiry that has never really settled despite exhausting all leads (for now). Of the thirty vessels named here, two had the name *City of New York* at some point in their lifetime, neither of them during the era of the *Titanic* sinking.

The accounts of these ships begin with key information about the vessels, and, for clarity, the details of the owners, tonnage and length are as they were at the time the ships were involved in the story of the *Titanic*. Over the years these vessels had multiple owners and operators and in some cases were renamed and heavily modified.

Each of these ships were also the subject of challenging situations, with evacuations, troop transporting, rescue missions, wartime service, collisions and minor groundings just some of the events that ships were involved in during their lifetime. While none of these ships were particularly unlucky, each one had its own unique story and may have suffered some tragic consequences along the way. However, that was the reality of shipping at the time and today there are many safety rules, regulations and equipment so that man-overboard issues are few and far between (although this is not to say they don't still happen). Sophisticated chart data fed with a global positioning system vastly reduces the risk of ships running aground, and, of course, the days of being sunk by a U-boat are well and truly over.

In any version of events there are always other elements that make the story what it is. In the case of the pride of the White Star Line it is the ships contained in this book, which for once will receive the credit they deserve. Each of the ships written about could quite easily fill a book, but here a brief rundown of each significant ship is given, along with details of their involvement in the timeline of events around the sinking of *Titanic*, a focus on their careers and where they finished up at the end of their lives.

These are the ships of the *Titanic* story.

1

Titanic

Type	Ocean liner
Length	882.5 feet
Gross tonnage	46,328
Built	Harland & Wolff, Belfast
Owners	White Star Line

So much has been written about *Titanic* that trying to condense the ship's story into one chapter is challenging as so many aspects are both sensational and interesting.

At a dinner party in 1907, the head of the White Star Line, Joseph Bruce Ismay, and the chairman of Harland & Wolff shipbuilding in Belfast, Lord Pirrie, discussed the possibility of creating three magnificent liners that would eclipse the nearest rivals of the Cunard Line, the newly built *Lusitania* and *Mauritania*. Agreements were made, plans were drawn up and construction began on *Olympic* and then *Titanic*, with the third sister to be built further down the line and named *Britannic*.

Less than a year later, on 31 May 1911, the four-funnelled marvel *Titanic* was launched. The luxuries on board rivalled those of the finest hotels in the world and her First Class passengers were anticipated to be the cream of society and members of the upper class. Sea trials took just a few hours outside Belfast Lough, and she arrived in Southampton on 4 April 1912 to prepare for her maiden voyage. Her captain was sixty-two-year-old Edward John Smith, a resident of Southampton who was due to retire after this final voyage, a magnificent end to a long career at sea with the White Star Line. The next week was spent taking on stores, preparing the cabins and loading precious coal into the holds down below, coal which had to be taken from other nearby ships due to a strike.

On Wednesday 10 April 1912, *Titanic* slipped her lines and was officially underway, crowds cheering from the jetty and passengers frantically waving back as the ship was slowly eased out of her berth. A near disaster occurred just moments later as the ship passed other vessels berthed around the corner; suction caused SS *New York* to be pulled towards *Titanic* so hard that the mooring lines broke and the stern of the smaller liner swung out. The quick reactions of the tug crews prevented a collision, and after a brief pause *Titanic* was on her way once again.

That night *Titanic* anchored in the harbour at Cherbourg where tenders brought out passengers and mail. It was the same the following morning off the Irish harbour of Queenstown, the liner too big to enter so anchoring just off the coast. On 11 April, she weighed anchor and headed west with 2,200 people on board, expected to arrive at her final

Titanic and *Olympic* in Belfast.

destination of New York within a week. The onlookers stood on the shore at Queenstown were the last people to photograph *Titanic* afloat.

The following few days were uneventful for the passengers who were entertained by the ship's band or enjoyed the library, smoking room, Café Parisien or perhaps the Turkish baths. Down below, the crew were working hard running the ship as well has having to deal with a fire in one of the coal bunkers which burned for several days before eventually being extinguished. As *Titanic* was now in the Mid-Atlantic in April the ice warnings were coming in thick and fast to the Marconi radio room, signals warning of potential dangers ahead. However, late in the night of 14 April these warnings were to be of huge significance as, at 2340 hours, the lookouts rang the bell in the crow's nest and reported an iceberg dead ahead.

First Officer William Murdoch attempted to carry out evasive manoeuvres. However, the ship had no chance of stopping and instead her starboard side was heavily damaged as the ice scraped down the hull, opening up hull plating and allowing water into the first five of sixteen watertight compartments. Originally, the builders had designed the ship to remain afloat with the first three of these compartments flooded with water, but with four or five flooded this was not viable. In addition, as the top of the watertight bulkheads only went so high, the resulting water ingress would simply spill over into the next compartment as the bow was weighed down further. The builders had said the ship was 'practically unsinkable', but the press had conveniently discarded the 'practically' part in their newspaper reports which led to many having the false notion that *Titanic* was indestructible. Designer Thomas Andrews was on board to check the damage and make an assessment. His analysis was clear when he reported back to the captain – the ship was going to sink.

Board of Trade safety regulations stipulated that every ship over 10,000 tons had to have sixteen lifeboats, but nobody thought to mention that *Titanic* was over four times that size and sixteen lifeboats (plus four additional collapsible boats that were held nearby) would only hold around half of the people on board. This was just one major blunder that the ship now had to face the consequences of.

The lifeboats were swung out and began to be filled, officially with women and children first. Only one was filled to maximum capacity and one left the ship with just twelve people on board when it could have held around sixty. As the bow slowly went down, the urgency of the situation became more apparent, panic starting to set in as the stern rose up. Eventually, all the lifeboats were away, with at least one floating off *Titanic* and capsizing. Suddenly, the power on board failed, plunging the ship into darkness. As the aft end of the liner rose high into the air, the funnels cracked off and the ship broke in half. At 0220 hours on Monday 15 April 1912, the grandest ship in the world slipped beneath the cold Atlantic waves.

The lifeboats now had to await rescue, and those people left in the water succumbed to the freezing temperatures within minutes. By the time the Cunard liner *Carpathia* reached

Titanic in Southampton. (Painting by Stuart Williamson)

the scene just over two hours later there was very little evidence that a huge disaster had taken place. Just 705 survivors were rescued, meaning over 1,500 people had perished. The exact figure would always be disputed but 1,512 names are listed on the Belfast memorial opened on the hundredth anniversary of the disaster.

There were two inquiries into the loss of *Titanic*, an American one and a British one. Each scrutinised the events leading up to the sinking, and the testimonies of the survivors so soon after the event led to the story being in the papers for months afterwards. A nearby ship, the *Californian*, had been stopped in ice and had seen distress rockets at the time of the sinking but had done nothing. Ice reports had been transmitted to every ship in the area warning of the dangers of the bergs, yet *Titanic* had continued to send personal traffic for the wealthy passengers. The speed was not reduced and the lifeboats were launched barely half full.

A raft of new laws and regulations were brought in after the sinking of *Titanic*, not least the ability to save every person on board a ship if it came to grief. More lifeboats, lifejackets, twenty-four-hour radio watch and the International Ice Patrol were just some of the lessons learned.

In the meantime, the cable ship *Mackay-Bennett* was despatched to recover the hundreds of bodies that were now floating in the Atlantic. The ship recovered over 300 bodies, many of which were buried in Halifax, Nova Scotia. Three other ships would head out in the search for bodies, each one coming back with fewer than the one before. The outbreak of the First World War led to the story of *Titanic* receding in people's minds for many years until the publication of the book *A Night to Remember*, by Walter Lord, in 1955 retold the story with the help of sixty survivors. It was so popular that it was made into a film starring Kenneth More in 1958.

Titanic sinking in the early hours of 15 April 1912.

The wreck of *Titanic* would not be found for seventy-three years, a joint French-American expedition beginning the search in the summer of 1985. After a disappointing search by sonar, the French passed the baton to American oceanographer Dr Robert Ballard who, in the last few days of the search, successfully located the wreck of the world's most famous ship. He not only proved that *Titanic* was upright and broken in two, but that the position of the ship was 13 miles away from where she had radioed in the distress calls back in 1912. The discovery made headlines across the globe and Ballard was immediately given funding for a second expedition a year later. On this occasion, he brought along a manned submersible named *Alvin* and a remotely operated vehicle (ROV) named *Jason Junior* to get more detailed views of the wreck.

The team brought back some incredible first photos of the ship, specifically a chandelier in the Grand Staircase and an unlocked safe in the debris field. The wreck was in two halves 2,000 yards apart, separated by thousands of items that had spilled from the ship during the sinking. The team vowed to leave the wreck site undisturbed, instead laying a memorial plaque on the hull before departing. However, in 1987, the French half of the first expedition team returned to salvage hundreds of artefacts from the wreck site and continued to do so for many more years. These items were later displayed in exhibitions around the world with tiny pieces of coal sold as souvenirs to a public eager for anything to do with *Titanic*.

The enthusiasm increased further in 1997 when film director James Cameron released his big-budget masterpiece *Titanic*, starring Kate Winslet and Leonardo DiCaprio. The film was an instant success and not only broke all box office records but won eleven Oscars. The hundredth anniversary of the disaster in 2012 garnered further coverage in the media and Cameron's film was reshown in cinemas fifteen years after its first release. By this point there was nobody left alive who remembered the ship itself. The final survivor, Millvina Dean, had died in 2009; she was just nine weeks old when placed into a lifeboat with her mother and brother.

Today, *Titanic* is synonymous with disaster, yet so many forget this. The countless books and documentaries cover the same old ground and the tasteless souvenirs lead the public today to be less affected by the fact that 1,500 people died a terrible death in the cold Atlantic and that the trauma and loss felt by the survivors and relatives affected generations of their families. Memorials to *Titanic* can be found in most major cities on both sides of the Atlantic, especially in places directly associated with the ship: London, Southampton, Liverpool, Belfast, New York, Washington DC, Cherbourg and Cork. There are also smaller tributes and plaques in towns and villages.

One thing is certain, the story of *Titanic* and the people on board her will never be forgotten, not least since the events of 2023 with the loss of a tourist submersible near the wreck that cost five lives and once again put *Titanic* back in the headlines.

2

Olympic

Type	Ocean liner
Length	882.5 feet
Gross tonnage	46,328
Built	Harland & Wolff, Belfast
Owners	White Star Line
Link to *Titanic*	Sister ship

Following the dinner party in 1907, when the idea of the three sister ships had been conceived, the green light was given to proceed with the building of these liners, the first of which was *Olympic*. While the plans for the ships were identical, there were just a few differences between them that meant that an eagle-eyed expert could tell them apart.

The most obvious difference was that *Titanic*'s promenade deck was enclosed whereas *Olympic*'s was open to the sea air. However, from a distance it was very difficult to tell them apart without this knowledge, many of the slight differences being internal. Construction started on the ship, known simply as Yard 400, and before long both ships were towering over the Belfast skyline side by side. There were 15,000 workers on each ship, hammering rivets into the hull plating and slowly constructing what could only be viewed as a skyscraper that would soon slide gracefully into the harbour.

It was a White Star tradition that their ships were not launched with champagne. Therefore, on the day of the launch, 20 October 1910, it was just a case of the ship being greased up and pushed backwards until the chains took hold and slowed the ever-increasing speed until *Olympic* was towed away into her fitting-out basin. Here the boilers, fittings and funnels were added over the following seven months.

Olympic sailed from Belfast on 31 May 1911, the same day that *Titanic* was launched. She departed on her maiden voyage on 14 June, meeting with a fanfare of cheers from the crowds lining Southampton docks. The largest ship in the world left England and headed out to sea for the first time with paying passengers, calling at Cherbourg and Queenstown along the way. Her voyages were usually uneventful, the luxury of the ship keeping the passengers entertained during the crossings. Many of them were frequent travellers and willing to pay the vast amounts for the staterooms, suites and cabins that were on offer. However, it was the Third Class passengers that brought in a lot of the money for White Star, their liners in effect being emigrant ships transporting hundreds of Irish, French and Scandinavians looking to start a new life in the US.

It was not long before *Olympic* met with an incident that would have an outward ripple on her story for years to come. On 20 September 1911, the liner was transiting the Solent on

Olympic in 1929.

her fifth voyage under the command of Captain Edward John Smith and running parallel to the nearby warship HMS *Hawke*. The Edgar class cruiser, which had been launched in 1891, was 387 feet long, not even half the length of the *Olympic*, but now suddenly *Hawke* was met with the liner turning to starboard without warning and this left the cruiser with no time or space to take avoiding action. The bow of *Hawke* sliced into the starboard side aft of *Olympic*, the warship's bow being built to withstand the damage caused by ramming and sinking enemy vessels.

The damage to the two ships was vast. *Olympic* had a huge hole both above and below the waterline running up several decks and *Hawke*'s bow had been completely crumpled. Incredibly, there were no lives lost but the two ships had to be taken away to be repaired. It was two weeks before *Olympic* was sufficiently patched up to head back to Belfast, where repairs took another six weeks on top of that. During that time work was slowed down on finishing *Titanic*, which was still being fitted out, as Harland & Wolff rushed to get the damaged sister ship back in service.

Following the sinking of *Titanic* in 1912, it became apparent that *Olympic* had responded to distress messages but was hundreds of miles away at the time and would have never made it there before other ships. The fallout from the lack of lifeboats on *Titanic* led to many crew members walking off the ship until safety was improved. The situation worsened when dozens of strikers mutinied and refused to work, the ship's sailings being cancelled, and many workers ended up in court. The judges found that the case against the workers was proven but they were not given a sentence due to the bad publicity that the White Star Line was receiving and the fact that the public were on the side of the crew members. Eventually, the dispute was resolved and the ship sailed once again. Months passed and it was not until later that year, during a refit, that the lifeboats were increased from twenty to sixty-eight.

Two years after the *Titanic* sinking the First World War broke out. The cruiser *Hawke* had been repaired after the *Olympic* collision and had a brand-new bow. However, just three years later she became one more victim of the U-boat menace that was now plaguing the coast of Britain when she was sunk in a torpedo attack. *Olympic* took on a number of new wartime roles, starting with ferrying regular fare-paying passengers from Europe to the US to escape the dangers of the conflict. This was not to be for long as once again the liner made headlines when, on 27 October 1914, the King George V class battleship HMS *Audacious* struck a mine off the coast of Ireland and began to sink. *Olympic* was one of the ships that came to her rescue and when it was clear that the warship was going to be lost, the crew were transferred over to several ships in the area, *Olympic* taking on many of her Ship's Company and landing them at Belfast. Several photographs of the crippled *Audacious* taken by those watching the drama aboard *Olympic* were later released. The battleship eventually sank, and the wreck is a popular dive site today.

In the meantime, *Olympic*, along with her Cunard rivals *Aquitania* and *Mauritania*, were requisitioned by the Admiralty to be used as troop ships. The war was escalating and the need for manpower in France, Belgium and the Mediterranean meant that ships which could hold thousands of people were urgently required. Painted in a dazzle scheme of camouflage, the ships now held the prefix HMT and over the next few years they served their country well. As the US entered the war the ships were soon tasked with helping to bring thousands of American troops across the Atlantic to Europe, a straightforward job for these four-funnel liners.

Olympic passing *Nantucket Lightship* on a previous voyage before the collision.

For the U-boats a liner of this size would be a perfect target, not only in terms of hitting the enemy hard but also propaganda purposes. On 7 May 1915, the submarine *U-20* torpedoed and sank the Cunard liner *Lusitania*, sister to *Mauritania*, with devastating results. Only 13 miles off the south coast of Ireland, the liner went down in just eighteen minutes with the loss of 1,197 passengers and crew on board. For *Olympic* this would be reversed when, on 12 May 1918, the surfaced German submarine *U-103* was sighted in the English Channel while the liner was full of US troops heading to France. The crew of *Olympic* opened fire on the submarine and then the captain turned the ship towards *U-103* which by now was trying to crash-dive. It was too late and *Olympic* slammed into the conning tower just as the boat vanished beneath the surface, forcing the crew to resurface and scuttle the submarine. A nearby warship picked up survivors as the liner carried on towards Cherbourg without stopping.

During the war, *Olympic* carried around 201,000 troops, earning her the nickname 'Old Reliable' by those who both served and travelled on her during this time. Her captain, Bertram Hayes, earned a knighthood for his war service and a DSO (Distinguished Service Order) for sinking the U-boat.

After the war, *Olympic* returned to her passenger-carrying duties for the White Star Line but the Great Depression hit the shipping companies hard. By the early 1930s, the number of passengers on board was slowly declining and serious consideration had to be given to viability of running such a ship that was now over two decades old.

In the meantime, *Olympic* met with disaster off the US coast while under the command of Captain John Binks on 15 May 1934. She was heading west in heavy fog when the liner struck *Nantucket Lightship LV-117* with the loss of seven of her crew. The four survivors were rescued and taken on board the liner as quickly as possible. There was nothing they could do for the other vessel, and the badly damaged lightship sank.

Less than a year after the *Nantucket* disaster it was decided that *Olympic* should retire from service, her passenger numbers now so low and the White Star Line being forced to merge with Cunard to become the Cunard White Star Line. *Olympic* was laid up in Southampton in 1935 before she was towed away to be taken apart over the next two years for scrap, which took place at Inverkeithing on the River Forth.

Today, relics from *Olympic* are still in circulation. The White Swan Hotel in Alnwick has wooden panels and a staircase from the ship, the cruise liner *Millennium* has fixtures on board in their RMS *Olympic* Restaurant and the famous Honour and Glory feature that held a clock at the top is now on display in Southampton's SeaCity Museum. Although the ship is long gone, her legacy continues in these cherished artefacts. Her captain at the time of the sinking of *Titanic*, Herbert Haddock, is buried in St Mary Extra Cemetery in Sholing, Southampton.

Olympic may be long gone, but for fans of this ship and her incredible story she will always be known as 'Old Reliable'.

3

Britannic

Type	Ocean liner
Length	882 feet
Gross tonnage	48,158
Built	Harland & Wolff, Belfast
Owners	White Star Line
Link to *Titanic*	Sister ship

The stories of *Titanic* and *Olympic* can be linked closely together to some degree because they were a few hundred miles away when disaster happened, they were together in build and when *Titanic* was fitting out *Olympic* was in for repairs after the *Hawke* collision. The third sister ship was launched in 1914 from the same slipway but had no real connection to *Titanic* other than it being an almost identical ship, for *Titanic* was long gone by the time her sister was built.

There have always been rumours that *Britannic* was meant to be called *Gigantic* and that this was changed due to the naming being considered inappropriate after the disaster, but this is not true. Why some advertisements cropped up with that name on is anybody's guess, but official documentation issued long before this clearly dispels that rumour.

Britannic was going to be different in many ways and in particular the safety aspect was high on everybody's priority list by now, nobody wanting a repeat of anything on the scale of the *Titanic* disaster or of another workers' mutiny because of a lack of lifeboats. A new and improved lifeboat launching system was pioneered on *Britannic*, comprising huge gantries that could carry six lifeboats each fitted to the upper deck, resembling oversized cranes. Considering the *Lusitania* had major issues launching lifeboats when she was sunk in 1915 as the ship heeled over, this entire fit was based on the ship being in a stable condition during foundering as *Titanic* was.

However, *Britannic* was never destined to carry fare-paying passengers, her launch from Harland & Wolff on 26 February 1914 coming at a time when the situation in Europe was very tense, eventually culminating in the outbreak of the First World War in August. At this point, *Britannic* was still being fitted out. It was soon realised that these huge liners could be used for war service as thousands of people soon found themselves being called up to fight in the trenches of Belgium, France and Gallipoli. While *Olympic* was ferrying troops around, *Britannic* was finally called up to become a hospital ship on 13 November 1915, a role that many other ships had already been assigned but few were of such a size.

Bow of the *Britannic*.
(Painting by Stuart Williamson)

Unlike her sister ships, *Britannic*'s role now meant that any luxuries were no longer necessary. Every space was needed for beds and operating theatres, storage for items that were required to save lives and accommodation for the nurses and personnel that would help *Britannic* fulfil her role to the best of her ability. It was not long before she was departing Liverpool painted white with the standard green stripe running the length of the ship with red crosses at intervals to advertise to any passing enemy ship or submarine that she was not a ship of war but a ship of medical emergency.

This did not stop attacks on hospital ships throughout the war as names like *Asturias* hit the headlines (she suffered two torpedo attacks although the first one did not explode, the second two years later killed dozens). HMHS *Britannic* was now doing journey after journey continuously between Britain and the Mediterranean, picking up the wounded from the Greek islands in the Aegean Sea and then making the journey back as fast as possible. She did this successfully five times, but eventually her luck ran out.

On 21 November 1916, *Britannic* was heading through the Kea Channel off Greece under the command of Captain Charles Bartlett, who had actually moved *Titanic* during her building period into dry dock and now found himself steering the sister ship towards her next mission. Suddenly, a massive explosion rocked the ship. A minefield had recently been laid in the area and the liner was now holed and taking in water. Thankfully, because the journey was inbound to the war zone there were not thousands of wounded people to evacuate. However, with 1,065 people still on board the extra huge lifeboat gantries would now be used for real as *Britannic* was going down fast.

The crew got to work and the lifeboats were swung out and lowered while Captain Bartlett attempted to run the ship aground on the nearby island of Kea, although this failed due to the speed at which the huge liner was sinking. Also, there was another reason that the ship was going down faster than expected. The rules stated that portholes had to be closed during wartime transit work, but the heat on board meant that many people opened them anyway. This was now helping the ship sink quicker as row after row of open windows let the seawater flood through to the lower decks.

Nobody was killed in the explosion and the evacuation of *Britannic* was successfully carried out. Thirty-five lifeboats full of people were lowered and everybody on board was taken away from the ship. However, the evacuation took a horrendous turn very quickly when the bow of *Britannic* sank lower and the stern began to rise out of the sea. With the ship's engines still running, the propellers were turning even as they lifted out of the water and became deadly hazards to those in the vicinity of them. Two lifeboats full of survivors drifted into the churning props with the huge blades smashing the boats up into matchwood, instantly killing thirty people, who became the only victims of the *Britannic* sinking. Those aboard the nearby boats could only watch in horror and there was nothing any of them could do to halt this chain of events. All that was left was the remains of the lifeboats floating around the stern.

Within one hour the largest ship in the world had gone, a situation White Star Line had had to contend with twice in four years. The survivors were rescued by nearby ships that had come to *Britannic*'s assistance after the distress call was initially sent, although the bodies of many of her victims were never recovered.

In 1975, the legendary ocean explorer Jacques Cousteau found the wreck of *Britannic*. For the first time in six decades attention was again focused on the forgotten sister ship of *Titanic* when he returned the following year with his camera equipment. On board his research ship *Calypso*, the converted naval vessel that was well-known from his TV shows about diving and oceanography, were a number of survivors of the lost ship who were now seeing footage of the wreck for the first time. Filming for a documentary, he asked around the table if they thought it was a torpedo or a mine that had sunk them, most of them strongly believing it was a torpedo.

Britannic. (Painting by Stuart Williamson)

In 1995, *Titanic* discoverer Robert Ballard went to the wreck site, the first visitor since Cousteau, and uncovered brand-new information about the wreck that Cousteau had been unable to extract with the limited technology of the 1970s. The initial image of the wreck on the seabed with a huge hole in the side of her port bow simply wasn't accurate. The hole in fact was a huge crack down the side of the ship caused by the bow being detached from the rest of the hull as the liner's bow dug into the seabed while sinking before the ship would come to rest on her starboard side in around 400 feet of water. The wreck was in excellent condition, her four funnels long gone but the main hull a breathtaking sight as Ballard's team guided ROVs as well as the nuclear-powered research submarine *NR-1* over the remains for a television documentary that would be shown worldwide.

Today, the wreck of *Britannic* is owned by Simon Mills, an expert on the ship who has published several books on her history. There have been a number of major diving expeditions since Ballard last visited with new details emerging about the inner workings of the ship. High-definition photographs and video footage have provided an incredible insight into this remarkably preserved lost ship, although getting further into the wreck is still something that is to be done, with permission from the Greek government who monitor the dives in their waters.

It is now agreed that *Britannic* was indeed sunk by a mine, laid by *U-73* just one month before the sinking. The minefield claimed another ship nearby not long after, and this is also an incredible dive that has featured in several diving magazines and articles over the years. Despite being known for many years as *Titanic*'s forgotten sister, *Britannic* is very much a famous shipwreck in her own right these days and can no longer be classed as forgotten. An eponymous low-budget film about the disaster starring Jacqueline Bisset was produced in 2000 and there have been a number of fascinating books and diving magazine articles published as well as a variety of documentaries.

The Merchant Navy Memorial at Tower Hill in London lists all those mariners who have no grave but the sea. Among the hundreds of vessels named on the memorial is that of HMHS *Britannic*, as well as the eighteen people whose bodies were never recovered. This magnificent ship never fulfilled her purpose as a passenger liner but instead served her country at a time of war and brought home those who thought they would never return. For that alone, *Britannic* served her country well.

HMHS *Britannic* at Moudros during her war service.

4

Carpathia

Type	Ocean liner
Length	558 feet
Gross tonnage	13,555
Built	Swan & Hunter, Wallsend
Owners	Cunard Line
Link to *Titanic*	Rescue ship

One of the most important ships in the entire story of the *Titanic* is a much smaller liner owned by the rivals to White Star, the Cunard liner *Carpathia*. She would go down in history as the only ship to rescue the survivors of the disaster, an act of humanity that led to her captain being awarded honours, medals, trophies and being immortalised in Hollywood. What should have been a workhorse for the transatlantic and Mediterranean services ended up being one of the most famous ships in the world.

Built at the C. S. Swan and Hunter yard in Wallsend, *Carpathia* was launched on 6 August 1902 with a capacity of around 1,700 passengers. This was later increased to over 2,500 in three classes, the majority of them in Third Class cabins, and upped her overall tonnage slightly too.

On the night of 14 April 1912, *Carpathia* was heading east across the Atlantic on a journey that had started at New York three days earlier and would end in Fiume, Austria-Hungary, in a week's time. The sea was freezing cold and, like many ships, the radio reports broadcast warned of the ice that the ship had passed on her travels. Captain Arthur Rostron was a Southampton man who had been at sea for many years and on this night he had turned in and was asleep when radio operator Harold Cottam also decided to head to his own cabin. As he was getting undressed, Cottam put his headset back on to see if there was anything interesting in the airwaves. He had heard nothing but ice reports and personal traffic from *Titanic* all evening, but this small decision would change not only his life, but hundreds of others. He stopped for a second as he tried to comprehend what he was hearing – distress calls from the largest ship in the world.

Writing down what he heard, he raced into the captain's cabin and startled him awake. For a second, the commanding officer was raging but then realised that something was seriously wrong as the details were conveyed to him. As Rostron read the message, he immediately ordered the ship to turn around and head to the site of the sinking, a position that put them around 54 miles away, making *Carpathia* the closest ship to respond at this point. They could be there in around four hours.

Carpathia in New York.

The crew braced themselves for what could be a major sea disaster. A ship of that size going down in these bitter conditions could only mean certain deaths. Nobody could survive for any length of time, and that is without the knowledge of the lack of lifeboats on board. *Carpathia*'s engineers were told that the captain required 'every ounce of steam' they could produce. The passengers were woken up and prepared for the sudden influx of potentially hundreds of survivors.

At around 0430 hours the *Carpathia* was in the rough area of where the *Titanic* was reported to have gone down. The first lifeboat was sighted and the pathetic remnants of the 2,200 passengers and crew started to drift into view. By now it was clear that the disaster was worse than expected as each boat highlighted how few people had survived.

After around four hours of hard work the survivors were hauled onto the upper deck. Children were placed in mail sacks and hoisted up and the frozen women still in their nightgowns were helped aboard. A total of 705 people were found alive, some survivors having left the ship alive only to succumb to the extreme cold while awaiting rescue.

Some of *Carpathia*'s passengers managed to take photographs of the lifeboats as the rescue operation was in full swing. These images showed the world just how harrowing the disaster became as so few of these boats were even there to be rescued. They noted the single lifeboat that had just twelve people on board when it had room for sixty-five.

By now the Cunard liner had hundreds of people on board, mostly women and children but also a few men and members of the crew. All of them were anxiously searching for their relatives, husbands, friends and colleagues. However, *Carpathia* could offer them nothing but false hope as it was revealed that there were no more survivors.

Once Rostron was satisfied that the ship had done all it could, the *Carpathia* headed west and made for New York. By now news of the sinking had reached land and the newspapers wanted a story. However, for three days *Carpathia* was silent as she made her way through lightning and a thunderstorm heading back to land. On the evening of 18 April the ship slowly make her way towards the city, and not a word was said on the airwaves from the ship. Press reporters hired boats to try and be the first to get the stories, heading out to the ship and shouting through megaphones, but again to no avail.

Carpathia confused everybody as she sailed straight past Cunard's Pier 54 and instead stood by White Star's empty pier where *Titanic* should have berthed. This is where the reality hit home for those watching as the *Titanic*'s lifeboats were lowered from *Carpathia* and handed over to their owners. *Carpathia* was then turned back around and came alongside 54. Here the photographers' flashes captured the first details of the survivors waiting to disembark in the torrential rain that had failed to keep the crowds away in what was the biggest news story in their lifetime.

The shocking images of the people coming down the gangway filled the news stories, the radio operator being carried due to his feet still being frozen. People staggered onto the jetty realising that they now had nothing left as all their possessions and identification had been lost just days before. For some they were now all alone in a huge city with nobody to turn to and nowhere to go.

However, *Carpathia* still had a job to do. Once everybody was safely ashore Rostron departed New York and headed back out to sea to continue the journey that had been interrupted just days before.

For his actions in co-ordinating the only rescue of the survivors, Captain Arthur Rostron was celebrated on both sides of the Atlantic as a hero of the sea. The crew were awarded special bronze medals that were made for them with the image of their ship on. Rostron was given a gold medal and a silver cup was presented to him by *Titanic* survivor Molly Brown, who had already gone down in legend as 'The Unsinkable Molly Brown' after taking charge of the lifeboat she was in. For Rostron it did not end there, and he was knighted by King George V and continued to receive awards and recognition for his efforts.

Carpathia carried on her service until the end of the First World War, being used to ferry troops across the Atlantic. On 17 July 1918, she was on a voyage from Liverpool to Boston with 166 crew and fifty-seven passengers when the German submarine *U-55* sighted her. Being part of a convoy, six other ships were nearby after a much larger convoy had split

Carpathia unloads *Titanic* lifeboats upon her arrival in New York.

in two earlier in the day; by now the ships were two days into the voyage and in the area known as the Southwest Approaches.

The U-boat fired a torpedo at *Carpathia* and this slammed into her port side. A second hit the engine room, killing five of her crew and leaving the stricken ship now doomed. Captain William Prothero, who had been in command for two years, ordered signals to be sent out warning the rest of the fleet which then fled at maximum speed and managed to escape. However, *Carpathia* was evacuated and the remaining 218 people on board were rescued. A third torpedo led to a huge explosion and the ship went down less than two hours after first being attacked.

The story of the heroic rescue of *Titanic*'s passengers and crew by the *Carpathia* has been acted out many times in films, in particular *A Night to Remember* and *Titanic*. Of those on board *Carpathia*, some told their stories to the press while others stayed silent. Captain Arthur Rostron became Commodore of the Cunard Line fleet in 1931 after being captain of some of the line's most magnificent ships, including the *Lusitania* before the war. On 4 November 1940, he died in the Wiltshire town of Chippenham after developing pneumonia aged seventy-one. He is buried at West End Churchyard in Southampton with his wife who died less than three years later. Today, he has a nearby street named after him as well as a tribute to him where his house stood on Chalk Hill.

In 1999, an expedition funded by author Clive Cussler's NUMA organisation (National Underwater and Marine Agency) was launched to find the wreck of *Carpathia*. After a false report of discovery, it turned out that what the team had found was the German liner *Isis*. A year later, another NUMA team was successful in the search and for the first time in eighty-two years *Carpathia* was looked upon by human eyes once again. Since then, a number of small items have been salvaged from the lost liner, which lies approximately 120 miles west of Fastnet. Today, the wreck is owned by Premier Exhibitions Inc. (formerly known as RMS Titanic Inc.) which made the salvage dives to *Titanic*.

Wreck of *Carpathia*. (Painting by Stuart Williamson)

5

Californian

Type	Ocean liner
Length	447 feet
Gross tonnage	6,223
Built	Caledon Shipbuilding & Engineering Co., Dundee
Owners	Leyland Line
Link to *Titanic* story	'The ship that stood still' while *Titanic* sank

If *Carpathia* and Arthur Rostron were the heroes of the story, the *Californian* and her captain have on many occasions been cast as the villains, perhaps unfairly so. The events of the night of 14/15 April 1912 have been pored over for more than a century with the benefit of hindsight to analyse what should have been done, what could have been done and what wasn't done. That said, the *Californian* went down in history as the ship that was closest to the sinking liner yet did nothing.

Built in Dundee at the Caledon Shipbuilding and Engineering Company, *Californian* was launched on 26 November 1901. She was intended to work as a cargo liner on transatlantic crossings, operating at a steady speed of around 12 knots. In addition to carrying approximately fifty-five crew, she could accommodate forty-seven passengers and at the time of her launch was the largest ship to be built in the town. As her primary role was for the cargo, the passengers on board would not expect to reach their destination quickly. However, the cabins on board were of a good standard and significantly cheaper than those on the faster and much larger ships.

In the late evening of 14 April 1912, *Californian* was on a voyage to New Orleans. It had started in London two weeks previously, an unscheduled stop as a result of storm damage which had delayed her slightly after originally sailing from Liverpool just days before. In command was Stanley Lord, a man who had taken over as captain just over a year before, and by 2220 hours that night he ordered the ship to stop engines due to the copious amounts of ice that was preventing the ship from safely transiting the area. After viewing the situation and realising that the ship could not make progress, he made the decision that *Californian* would commence the voyage again at first light. For now, there was very little anybody could do and so Captain Lord turned in for the night and went to bed.

Twenty-year-old Cyril Evans was the only wireless radio operator on board. Throughout the evening, he had been hearing the nearby ice reports and *Titanic*'s private traffic was particularly close by due to the increase in the noise. On one occasion Evans transmitted an ice report which almost blasted the ears of Jack Phillips, one of the two wireless

Californian as seen from *Carpathia* on the morning of 15 April 1912.

operators on board *Titanic*. His reply to the *Californian* was 'Shut up, shut up, I am busy, I am working Cape Race.' *Titanic* once again resumed their own traffic and, believing he had done his duty in passing the warning on, Evans packed his equipment up for the night and switched off the radio.

On the bridge Third Officer Charles Groves was on watch and noticed the lights of another ship far away in the distance. He informed Captain Lord as per protocol at around 2330 hours and he suggested to attempt to contact her by Morse lamp. This was tried without success. Around ten minutes later (the exact time the *Titanic* had stopped engines) the lights in the distance were seen to suddenly stop and then extinguish, coinciding with *Titanic* hitting the berg and the ship turning so that her lights were no longer exposed to anybody viewing from a distance.

The midnight watch took over and Second Officer Herbert Stone was now receiving a handover from Groves, who pointed out the lights on the horizon. Both of them now saw the ship and Stone then tried to contact it himself via the Morse lamp, again without success. At 0055 hours, rockets were seen coming from the mystery ship into the sky. Stone informed the captain who asked if they were company signals, but his reply was that he did not know.

Discussion and debate were thrown to and from the Officer of the Watch and the apprentice officer James Gibson, who had been carrying out the signalling. By around 0200 hours, the ship seemed to have gone and Gibson informed Captain Lord that they had fired eight white rockets in total and the ship now seemed to have departed.

At 0340 hours, the officers saw more rockets coming from another direction, but this was *Carpathia* firing them to let *Titanic* survivors know that they were there. By the time of the next watch being relieved it was clear that something wasn't right and at 0416 hours Chief Officer

George Stewart sighted the *Carpathia* in the distance. Around fifteen minutes later, Captain Lord woke and went out on deck to check the ice situation. By this point, Lord was getting concerned about the events of the night and so ordered the radio operator Cyril Evans woken up to find out if there was anything going on with that ship in the night. As Evans turned his equipment on the full horror of what had occurred just a few miles away struck home.

The airwaves were full of reports from various ships heading to the scene. Captain Lord ordered the ship to get underway immediately but by the time the *Californian* had managed to get to *Carpathia* all the survivors had been rescued. All that was left for *Californian* was a sea of wreckage, bodies and empty boats that had been cast adrift.

While the world showered the crew of *Carpathia* with medals and praise, the crew of *Californian* were vilified for their actions. At the two inquiries held in Britain and the US, radio operator Cyril Evans gave evidence about his actions that day. Needless to say, there was very little he could have done while asleep and being the only radio operator on board.

Captain Lord was summoned to give evidence at the American inquiry. However, by now newspapers were offering vast sums of money for the accounts of witnesses, who took the opportunity to make some cash and have their own stories in print. This led to conflicting reports in the press over how close the *Californian* was to the site of the sinking and the actions taken by the people on board that night. Even Lord's account tended to change from time to time and in the end few people could truly believe what was being said, whether it was a number of mistakes, miscalculations or barefaced lies.

While *Californian* was said to be around 19 miles from *Titanic*, both inquiries found that she must have been much closer due to the fact that they could see each other. However, the real shock came in 1985 when the wreck of *Titanic* was found 13 miles away from where she said she was. As a consequence, a new inquiry by the Marine Accidents Investigation Branch was set up in 1992 to look into whether *Californian* could have done anything after all. After examining the new evidence, the inquiry concluded that although the standards on board *Californian* that night and the crew's actions 'fell far short of what was needed', there was no way that *Californian* could have got to the scene of *Titanic*'s sinking before *Carpathia*.

Californian featured heavily in the film *A Night to Remember*, which opened the debate about the role Stanley Lord played and this has since been the subject of a number of books re-examining the evidence. Lord never cleared his name while he was alive and died at the age of eighty-four on 24 January 1962, going to his grave as the man who commanded the ship that stood by as 1,500 people died.

The only good thing to come out of this episode was that it became law for all ships to have a twenty-four-hour radio watch in case of emergency. When all was said and done, at no point did anybody on watch wake Evans to find out what was going on until it was too late.

Californian went back to sea as normal and a year later suffered a fire while alongside in Veracruz. The ship and her cargo were damaged, but she was repaired and put back in service again and was eventually requisitioned by the British government and placed on war service at the outbreak of the First World War. On 9 November 1915, while on a voyage from Salonica to Marseilles, she was hit by a torpedo from the German submarine *U-34* off Cape Matapan, Greece, which killed a fireman named Richard Harding. Despite efforts to tow her to safety, a second torpedo strike sent her to the bottom. Today, the wreck of *Californian* remains undiscovered.

6

Mesaba

Type	Cargo liner
Length	482 feet
Gross tonnage	6,833
Built	Harland & Wolff, Belfast
Owners	Atlantic Transport Line
Link to *Titanic*	Transmitted and received radio traffic on the night of the sinking

Now that the main ships involved in the story have been examined, the focus can switch to the less-well-known ships. Although these played a small part in the story, their input was vital and deserves to be detailed here.

Mesaba is one of the vessels that gets a brief mention in the story yet few know anything about her. Launched at Harland & Wolff in Belfast, the same as *Titanic*, on 11 September 1897, she was originally named *Winifreda* and owned by the Wilson & Furness-Leyland Line, but before being launched was purchased by the Atlantic Transport Line to replace ships taken over by the American government after the Spanish-American War. She had her maiden voyage in March 1898 and by June that year had run her last voyage for her owners before Atlantic Transport Line took over and she was renamed *Mesaba*.

She was mid-voyage off the coast of New York on 12 February 1899 when she came upon the steamer *Catania* in a ferocious storm, the ship struggling to stay afloat after flooding down below. The influx of water dampened the furnaces and left the ship stricken and rolling uncontrollably to the point where *Mesaba* was standing by to assist in the abandoning of the ship which was advised by the crew of *Mesaba*. However, *Catania*'s crew refused to leave and soon the two ships lost sight of each other as they were pounded by heavy waves and strong winds. After thirty-six hours of hell for her occupants, the *Catania* was able to make headway into New York under her own steam once again, her lifeboats having been swept away and leaving the crew unable to abandon ship even if they had wanted to. Thankfully, *Mesaba* had boats and had been close by if she was needed, but in the end, disaster was averted.

Six years later, in February 1905, *Mesaba* was once again involved in a mid-sea drama when a three-masted schooner named *Amanda* became weighed down by the sheer amount of ice that had built up on the ship. By the time the *Mesaba* sighted her she almost resembled an actual iceberg and was in danger of sinking if something wasn't done quickly. The sailing vessel was on a voyage from Newfoundland to Brazil with a cargo of dried fish and had managed to get as far as the Grand Banks when Captain Fitzgerald

A postcard featuring *Mesaba*.

and his seven crew realised that they were in a bad situation regarding the ice. Not only that, the ship had also started leaking not long after a storm had started to buffet the ship. The temperature plummeted and the few crew were working constantly just to keep the ship afloat. The cargo and any heavy equipment like cables and anchors were gathered together and thrown overboard to lighten the ship, and this went on for five days until the exhausted men were sighted by *Mesaba* on 1 February. The grateful crew were taken on board the rescue ship and Captain Fitzgerald set the schooner on fire so that it would sink and not be a hazard to navigation. The burning ship was later reported by several passing ships but by now the *Amanda*'s crew were out of danger and slowly recuperating on their way to New York.

However, this wasn't the end of this part of the story. The captain, chief officer, surgeon and four seaman were later that summer given awards by the Newfoundland government for services rendered to the wreck of the *Amanda*.

In 1906, *Mesaba* was once again in the papers when Madame Celine Dobres, who suffered with trachoma, was refused entry into the US. Upon reaching Ellis Island after her voyage, she informed the authorities that her husband and children were waiting for her. However, she was not even allowed to talk to them for a moment before being deported, heading to London on *Mesaba*, much to the outrage of those reading about this in the papers the following day. This was one of a number of scandals regarding American immigration during this period, and several more relating to other ships are mentioned in this book.

On the night of 14 April 1912, *Mesaba* was Mid-Atlantic on a usual crossing and encountering a lot of ice in the area, so much so that the crew felt it necessary to transmit warnings to other ships, as so many others in the area had also done over the last few days.

At 1950 hours that night, the wireless operator of *Mesaba*, Stanley Adams, transmitted the following:

> To Titanic
> In Lat. 42 N. to 41.25 Long 49 W to Long
> - 50.30 W saw much heavy pack ice and
> great number large icebergs also field ice.
> Weather good, clear

It was said that the message received from *Mesaba* never reached the bridge of *Titanic* and was instead lost within the piles of signals transmitted and received from fare-paying passengers. Like the other nearby ships, *Mesaba* heard the final transmissions from *Titanic* while racing to the scene of the sinking but being several hundred miles away she had no chance of reaching the site to be able to do any good.

When the British inquiry was held just two months later the *Mesaba* ice warning was brought up several times. Sir Robert Finlay of the White Star Line stated that if the message in question had reached the bridge, 'the disaster would never have happened', confident he was that this warning was the main important one. Chairing the inquiry, Lord Mersey stated that 'if they got that message on the bridge they were grossly careless', but still stated that again this particular message can't have been seen and so perhaps the officers were forgiven if they were unaware of the danger of this particular ice warning. This was backed up by Fifth Officer Harold Lowe and Second Officer Lightoller who stated that they had not been made aware of this message.

As with many other ships, *Mesaba* ended up on convoy duties during the First World War and a minor collision in the foggy Irish Sea with the steamship *Lizard* on 11 August 1918 led to an inquiry which apportioned blame to both parties.

In the chaos of the war *Mesaba* fell victim to the dreaded U-boat, like many other ships of her type. On 1 September 1918, with just over two months left of the war, she was in ballast as part of a convoy heading from Liverpool to Philadelphia when, just 21 miles from Tuskar Rock in St George's with ninety-eight crew on board, she was hit by a torpedo from the German submarine *U-118*. She went down quickly, her captain Owen Percy Clarke and nineteen of the crew losing their lives. The gunboat *Kildini* was nearby and helped rescue the survivors, an effort that led to Lieutenant F. J. Silva RNR being awarded the Liverpool Shipwreck and Humane Society medal for gallantry.

The story of *Mesaba*'s role in the *Titanic* saga has not been written about very much beyond the few questions at the inquiries. However, in 2022, it was announced that a survey of areas around the Irish Sea by the universities of Bangor and Bournemouth had found a number of lost ships on the seabed, 273 to be exact. Among these was the wreck of *Mesaba* broken in two, the SONAR image giving a fairly detailed view of the general condition of the ship, her bow twisted to one side as her stern remained seemingly upright.

For once it was *Mesaba*'s turn to be in the news. Perhaps one day soon underwater cameras will bring back footage of the wreck on the seabed and her story will once again capture the interest of the public, for the stories of ships like these deserve to be told.

7

Rappahannock

Type	Cargo ship
Length	370 feet
Gross tonnage	3,871
Built	A. Stephen & Son, Glasgow
Owners	Furness Withy & Co., Liverpool
Link to *Titanic*	Ice reports and false story of passing *Titanic*

Another ship that is rarely in the limelight in the *Titanic* story is the cargo vessel *Rappahannock*. She was built in Scotland by A. Stephen & Sons of Glasgow in 1893 for the transatlantic routes, carrying general cargo, and she did this for almost two decades before the *Titanic* disaster. On the days leading up to the disaster she was eastbound from Halifax, Nova Scotia, heading to Britain, but several conflicting stories emerge about the role this ship played in the events that followed.

Some versions of events that night claim that *Rappahannock* transmitted an ice warning on the night of Saturday 13 April, stating that the ship had just passed some ice, and that nearby *Titanic* had acknowledged the signal. Another says that it took place a good twenty-four hours later just before the *Titanic* struck the iceberg. Both accounts appear in two separate books, authored by different people (Walter Lord, and Jack Eaton and Charlie Haas).

However, what is interesting is that this was not mentioned at any inquiry and nor does anybody from the ship come forward to say that they were there or remember being near *Titanic* on the night in question. Indeed, the Board of Trade received a letter from the owners confirming that none of their ships were in the vicinity of the *Titanic* on that night. However, the ship allegedly passing *Titanic* sometime before the disaster is mentioned in Geoffrey Marcus's *The Maiden Voyage*, but with a lack of evidence this could be nothing more than pure speculation. One thing is certain, though, the *Rappahannock* was out at sea in the icy Atlantic on the night of *Titanic*'s sinking, even if she was too far away to be of assistance.

Rappahannock reached her destination on 20 April 1912, but very little was spoken of her being in the area at the time of the sinking. Where this all came from is unknown, but like much speculation about what happened that night and where the ships' exact positions were, we may never know the truth unless some new written evidence comes to light one day.

A year after the *Titanic* disaster, in October 1913, *Rappahannock* once again found herself close to a disaster when the Canadian passenger liner *Volturno*, of the Royal Line, was on fire in the Atlantic. When the distress calls came in, *Rappahannock* raced to the scene along with several other ships in the area. Captain Frederick Harnden later told the inquiry into the *Volturno* disaster that *Rappahannock* was 160 miles from the burning ship and had picked up the relay of the distress call from the Cunard liner *Carmania*. When *Rappahannock* arrived on the scene, the crew launched a lifeboat with nine volunteers on board to render assistance, one of them being the chief officer. It was the early hours of the morning of 10 October and the ship was by now burning out of control, yet this tiny boat managed to do several runs to and from the ship, bringing back fifteen women and four children when it eventually managed to get close enough. By the time it went back again to rescue more people, there were so many rescue boats now gathering around that *Rappahannock*'s boat couldn't get any closer. The ship tried to assist with spraying oil on the water to help calm the sea but after a few days *Volturno* was deliberately sunk as she posed a hazard to navigation. By now 136 people had lost their lives in the disaster.

Three years after the loss of *Volturno*, on 26 October 1916, the *Rappahannock* was on a voyage eastbound from Halifax to London under the command of Captain Richard Garrett. She was only 70 miles off the Isles of Scilly when the German submarine *U-69* sank her with the loss of all thirty-seven crew. As there were no survivors, she was officially listed as missing for several days until eventually a body washed ashore at Porranporth on the north-western edge of Cornwall on 8 November 1916. The body was soon identified as a man named Joannes Jacobus Theuwkens, a Belgian national who was a greaser on board *Rappahannock*. If confirmation was needed that the ship was lost, it came the day after when various pieces of cargo were found floating in the area by SS *Corinthian*. These items were positively identified as belonging to the missing *Rappahannock*.

On 27 January 1917, a German announcement stated that the U-boat had attempted to stop the ship and had sunk her but claimed that the crew all got away in a boat. Not one survivor was found. Today their names are listed on the Tower Hill merchant navy memorial in London.

8

Baltic

Type	Ocean liner
Length	729 feet
Gross tonnage	23,876
Built	Harland & Wolff, Belfast
Owners	White Star Line
Link to *Titanic*	Ice warnings transmitted and involved in rescue search

The 'Big Three' were not the only ocean liners that the White Star Line had in its long history. There were several other ocean liners that had just as interesting careers and were some of the largest ships in the world despite being overshadowed by the four-funnel giants.

One of these was *Baltic*, built at the Harland & Wolff shipyard and launched on 21 November 1903. Although she was not the fastest in comparison with her rivals, she was one of what were initially dubbed at the time the 'Big Four', comprising *Baltic*, *Cedric*, *Celtic* and *Adriatic*.

With a top speed of 19 knots, these ships could carry almost 3,000 passengers on the Liverpool to New York route. On her first voyage in 1904 *Baltic* did just that under the command of none other than Captain Edward John Smith, later captain of *Titanic*. An early incident with *Baltic* made the papers during a voyage with a full complement of passengers. On 9 May 1907, she ran aground off the coast of Sandy Hook, a barrier spit off New Jersey. She was trapped on the sand bank for twenty-four hours, one of the passengers on board being philanthropist Andrew Carnegie as well as many other famous and influential people of the time. The episode was a slight embarrassment for the White Star Line, but resulted in only a minor delay, minimal coverage in the press and no damage to the ship.

However, *Baltic* soon gained a reputation as a problem ship after suffering a number of minor mishaps including collisions, fires and breakdowns. This did not deter passengers from choosing *Baltic* to travel across the Atlantic, even when the most serious of the accidents involved a collision with the tanker *Standard* on 30 June 1910. There was significant damage to the ships but thankfully only one person from the tanker was injured. Once again, this incident occurred off Sandy Hook, the hazy weather at the time being a contributing factor, according to the captain. *Standard* was eventually brought into the port of Copenhagen after travelling across the Atlantic. The damage she had sustained in the collision later caused a fire on 19 July during the unloading of fuel. The subsequent explosion inflicted massive damage on the tanker and left two of the crew injured.

On 23 January 1909, *Baltic* was heading to New York on one of her regular voyages when suddenly her radio operator picked up a distress call from the White Star Liner *Republic*.

A postcard featuring *Baltic*, 1914. (Author)

The latter had been involved in a collision with the Italian steamship *Florida* off the coast of Nantucket. *Baltic* and a nearby ship named *Lorraine* swiftly responded and raced to the scene, as did many other ships that were in the immediate vicinity. *Florida* was able to start the rescue operation and soon had hundreds of *Republic*'s passengers and crew on board as the first rescue ships began to arrive on the scene. By now the two ships had drifted many miles apart but thankfully the sea was calm when *Baltic* began transferring the survivors from *Florida*. The story of the rescue operation and the heroic efforts of the wireless operator made headlines worldwide and *Baltic* was successful in rescuing the survivors from the *Florida*. *Republic* eventually went down but aside from the five people killed in the initial crash, everybody else was saved and *Baltic* later arrived in New York to a hero's welcome with over 1,000 extra personnel on board.

However, tragedy seemed to follow the *Baltic* around. In August 1911, the ship arrived in Queenstown, Ireland, to the news that a famer named John Looney had fallen into the water on the quay while he was waiting for the ship which was bringing his son home. The incident occurred at the White Star jetty at 0215 hours on a Saturday morning and following a search his body was found after several hours.

In September 1911, nine women were taken on board in New York. They were described as 'lunatics' being deported by the US authorities and had two nurses to accompany them on the crossing to Britain. Tragically, during the voyage, on Tuesday 26 September, one of them, forty-seven-year-old Irish woman Mary Dwyer, committed suicide by hanging herself in one of the steerage compartments. Her body was buried at sea, the simple alteration to the passenger lists giving minor details of her passing. *Baltic* arrived in Queenstown soon after where the remaining eight patients were landed.

On the night of 14 April 1912, *Baltic* was steaming across the Atlantic when her normal radio traffic was filled with reports of ice. Her radio operator transmitted the following to nearby *Titanic* in the hope that it would be useful: 'Greek steamer *Athenia* reports passing icebergs and large quantities of field ice today in latitude 41° 51' N, longitude 49° 52' W. Wish you and *Titanic* all success. Commander.' As *Titanic* hit the iceberg later that evening, *Baltic* received the SOS transmitted by her Marconi room. Like many of the ships nearby, she raced to the scene, being nine hours away, to lend a hand in a major disaster for the second time in three years. It is not known whether the crew of *Baltic*, as a White Star Liner, knew about the small number of lifeboats on board *Titanic*. Alas, *Baltic* was too far away to be able to do anything. The only positive outcome was to be the introduction of more lifeboats following the inquiries which would allow a ship of that size to be at sea with enough equipment for everybody to survive in the event of an emergency. *Baltic* had had its fair share of drama over the years and the loss of a ship like *Titanic* was a disaster waiting to happen.

In May 1913, *Baltic* was once again involved in a shipwreck when the liner *Haverford* ran aground off Queenstown. The ship's occupants were taken off successfully and *Baltic* was tasked with transporting fifty-three of them onwards to New York, while other liners assisted the remaining passengers.

At the outbreak of the First World War in 1914, *Baltic* initially continued with her normal role as a passenger ship along with the rest of her sister ships. However, this all changed in 1915 when she was requisitioned by the Admiralty to carry troops as fighting in the trenches of France and Turkey heated up. On 26 April 1917, she was attacked by the German submarine *U-66* which had been pursuing her for two days and during that time had attacked her several times with torpedoes. Incredibly, the U-boat failed in its mission and the ship escaped without a scratch, luckily for the people on board.

In the June of that year, *Baltic* was host to General John Pershing who was leading the first batch of American troops into the war after the US joined the conflict on the side of the Allies. This ten-day voyage made headlines for all the right reasons, and was such a significant event that a plaque was placed in the main hall on board the ship to commemorate it. She continued to transport troops right until the end of the war when 32,000 Canadians were brought over to France in 1918. At the end of the war *Baltic* was returned to her owners.

On 8 October 1921, *Baltic* was involved in another tragedy. When the ship departed Liverpool on a routine voyage, passenger Professor Edward Porritt fell overboard. Having had several works of a historic and political nature published and lectured at Harvard University for two years, the sixty-year-old had been visiting Lancashire. *Baltic* searched the River Mersey, but his body was never recovered.

On 9 June 1923, *Baltic* was proceeding once again from Liverpool to New York and two hours into the journey the bottom of the ship scraped an underwater obstacle just off the Irish coast. The White Star Line played down the incident, saying that there was very little damage and although she turned back to port, it was not serious enough to put into the nearest port. The passengers were unaware of any drama, one telling the *Daily Mail* that he was writing about Ireland on the starboard side but when he came back on deck shortly after he found that Ireland was now to port, the only knowledge of anything amiss the fact that the ship had turned around. On 13 June, after an inspection that proved only slight bending of plates, *Baltic* was given the all-clear to sail to New York and she departed that night four days late.

Immigration was a big issue during this period of American history and in November 1923 this was further highlighted when a woman was placed on board *Baltic*. Mary Brennan was to be deported after a journey to visit her wealthy aunt in New York was cut short by a standard visit to the Immigration Centre on Ellis Island. The eighteen-year-old was pregnant and intended to stay only until the baby was born, although this was not taken into account and nor was the fact she had plenty of money on her person at the time. She was sent away and was taken ill after contracting pneumonia during her time on Ellis Island.

On 15 November, she had the baby on board *Baltic* while out at sea but sadly the baby died two hours after being born and a few hours after that so did Mary. Both were buried at sea.

The curse of the *Baltic* struck again on 14 June 1925 after the ship had just left Queenstown heading to Liverpool on the final leg of a transatlantic voyage. A steward heard gunfire from Cabin 185 and raced there to find thirty-nine-year-old Robert Edward Howarth dead from a gunshot wound to the head having committed suicide. His body was taken ashore and buried in Lancashire several days later on 19 June.

On 1 August 1927, the *Baltic* arrived in Liverpool after another New York voyage and reported that the ship had accidentally rammed a whale off the southern Irish coast the day before. The collision had impaled the whale on the bow of the ship and tearing a huge hole in the 18-foot-long creature. The ship had to reverse engines to shake it free before being able to carry on with the voyage. In October the following year, *Baltic* found herself once again heading towards a ship in distress as the Dutch steamship *Celaeno* was in difficulties in a storm. Thankfully, the ship was able to make it to port without the need for assistance, although thanks were relayed to *Baltic* and nearby German liner *Albert Ballin*.

It wasn't all doom and gloom for the workhorse of the White Star Line, however. In a story that made the news at Christmas 1928 the ship's purser was due to play the role of Father Christmas but did not have a beard. An official jumped into a taxi and quickly headed to the shops in Liverpool but did not get back to the ship in time to catch the sailing, *Baltic* now heading down the Mersey and out to sea. A nearby tug raced to the ship where the false beard was hoisted up the side using a rope. Crisis averted!

On 6 December 1929, *Baltic* was involved in yet another rescue when the schooner *Northern Light* was in distress off Newfoundland during a severe gale. One of her crew of six, Rex Parsons, the son of the captain, had already drowned by being washed over the side of the vessel. *Baltic* was on hand to send out one of their lifeboats. A 50-foot line was thrown by their crew to the *Northern Light* and the remaining five crew members were taken on board *Baltic* and saved from certain death. This rescue did not go unnoticed as ten members of the crew of *Baltic* were awarded the Board of Trade Bronze Medal for Gallantry for this rescue. They were:

Frank Goodchild
George Meikle
Stephen Taws
James Walker
John Boylan
John Whelan
Peter Codd
William Williams
George Riley
John Roberts

Like many businesses during the Great Depression, financial hardship hit the liner industry and despite refits and upgrades *Baltic* was eventually sold on to Japanese ship breakers and scrapped in Osaka in 1933. In her lifetime of almost three decades this liner had been involved in many scrapes, hired for war service and had taken part in two of the most famous rescues in history. Therefore, *Baltic* is one ship that has been remembered and is well documented.

9

New York

Type	Ocean liner
Length	560 feet
Gross tonnage	10,508
Built	J. & G. Thomson, Clydebank
Owners	American Line
Link to *Titanic*	Near collision in Southampton as *Titanic* sailed past

SS *New York*'s near collision with *Titanic* went down in history as an omen after the *Titanic* sank just days later. The ship which almost stopped the grandest liner in the world from sailing started life as the Inman Line vessel *City of New York*. Launched on 15 March 1888, she had the capacity to carry over 1,700 passengers and 362 crew for the transatlantic route and held the record for the fastest eastbound crossing from August 1892 until the record was taken less than a year later.

Together with her sister ship *City of Paris*, *New York* was a twin-screwed steamship that sported three tall masts and three funnels crowded together near the midships section of the vessel. *City of New York* was christened by Lady Randolph Churchill, mother of future Prime Minister Winston Churchill, and just months later was already on her maiden voyage out of Liverpool. Her speed caused concern at the rival White Star Line and they launched *Teutonic* and *Majestic* soon after to counteract this.

Life on board *City of New York* was wonderful for those who had the ability to travel. She could carry 540 First Class, 200 Second Class and around 1,000 Steerage passengers. The facilities on board allowed passengers to relax and forget that they were even travelling by being waited on or retiring to the library to indulge in a book.

A change of ownership from the UK-based Inman Line to the American Line in 1893 meant that the *City of New York* was now an American ship. On 22 February 1893, the Stars and Stripes were hoisted by President Benjamin Harrison himself, and the ship was renamed simply *New York*. On 26 April 1898, *New York* was commissioned by the US government as an auxiliary cruiser for the Spanish-American War and renamed USS *Harvard*, now officially a naval vessel. On 4 July, while she was loaded with Prisoners of War, a guard opened fire on one of the prisoners who was attempting to flee. Panic spread among the rest of the prisoners and a full-scale riot was feared. This led to the troops shooting those who they believed were attacking them but in reality were probably quite confused about what was going on. Later known as the 'Harvard Incident', this event was eventually recognised as a case of simple miscommunication as a result of the language

New York's near collision with *Titanic* on 10 April 1912 in Southampton. (Unknown)

barrier, although six prisoners had been killed in the process. By September *Harvard* was back in the hands of her civilian owners who promptly put her in for a refit. Her engines were replaced, the number of funnels reduced to two and her name was changed back to *New York* once again.

On the morning of 10 April 1912, the ship was alongside in Southampton, berthed up against the White Star Liner *Oceanic*. Both ships were two of many that were not going anywhere anytime soon due to the coal strike that was crippling the shipping industry. At midday *Titanic*, loaded with coal taken from these surrounding ships, slipped her moorings and proceeded out of her berth and turned into Southampton Water on her maiden voyage, escorted closely by the tugs *Vulcan* and *Neptune*. With hundreds of passengers lining the upper decks a priest, Father Francis Brown, was among the crowd on *Titanic* and capturing this incredible ship on camera before he was due to depart the following day when the liner arrived at Queenstown. As the ship slowly made her way past the other ships, the suction that this huge liner created was too much for the cables holding *New York* to her mooring. The strain on these cables caused both *New York* and *Oceanic* to start moving and it was only a matter of time before the inevitable happened as the weight became too much for the lines to bear.

With a loud crack the lines parted and the stern of *New York* began to swing out towards the port side of *Titanic*, the passengers and other onlookers wide-eyed in horror as a disaster was unfolding right in front of them. Captain Smith immediately ordered the port propeller to reverse which began to turn the larger ship. At the same time, the tug *Vulcan* quickly swung into action to take *New York* away from the opposite side. This quick reactions of all the parties involved meant that the two ships came very close to collision but disaster was averted. Ironically, if they had collided, *Titanic* would not have been heading out on her disastrous maiden crossing and would instead, like her sister ship the

New York (as *City of New York*).

year before, have been making her way to Belfast for damage repairs. With only around an hour's delay, *New York* was pulled into the River Itchen and *Titanic* continued on her way.

Many people came to regard this incident as bad luck and even a terrible omen that should have been taken more seriously. Some felt so strongly about it that they departed the ship at Cherbourg and would not be persuaded to come back on board. One family on the ship were watched over at night-time by their mother while they slept. Seven-year-old Eva Hart remembered her mother Esther being awake while the rest of them were asleep and instead she would sleep during the daytime when she felt it was safer. Despite the heroic actions of the tugs and the handling of the situation by Captain Smith, there was still a lot of unease surrounding the *New York* incident in Southampton. It became a talking point for lots of people, many of them aware of the *Olympic/Hawke* collision the year before that had been caused by the same suction effect.

During the First World War *New York* was used once again called into military service as a troop transport and was renamed *Plattsburg*. On one voyage she suffered mine damage close to Liverpool, but other than that she survived to once again resume passenger-carrying service. In 1920, she was renamed *New York* yet again, this time with one less mast than before. She had only two more years in service when, after changing owners to the American Black Sea Line, she was sold for scrap and taken to Genoa where she was eventually broken up in 1923.

Despite all the incidents and headlines in her past, the only thing *New York* was remembered for was almost colliding with the ill-fated *Titanic* in Southampton.

10

Mackay-Bennett

Type	Cable ship
Length	270 feet
Gross tonnage	2,000
Builders	John Elder & Co., Glasgow
Owners	Commercial Cable Company
Link to *Titanic*	Recovery of victims after disaster

Of all the ships involved in the story of *Titanic*, *Mackay-Bennett* was one that not only had a unique job to do but this was a mission the ship was never designed to do. Launched in September 1884, she was named after the two people who founded the Commercial Cable Company, John Mackay and James Gordon Bennett (believed to be the origin of the exclamation 'Gordon Bennett').

The role of *Mackay-Bennett* was to lay and repair transatlantic cables, based mostly in the port of Halifax, Nova Scotia, on the American continent, and Plymouth, UK, on the European side. She made headlines in 1912 for the rescue of the crew members of the wreck of the sailing vessel *Caledonia* on 12 February. Little did the crew realise, but this was not the only shipwreck that *Mackay-Bennett* would be heavily involved with that year. Two months later the *Titanic* disaster shocked the world and the owners of the *Mackay-Bennett* soon received a request from the White Star Line.

After the sinking of *Titanic*, the owners began to charter a number of ships to search for the bodies of the 1,500 or so who had died on the ship and were potentially floating around the Mid-Atlantic in a huge sea of wreckage. Captain Frederick Harold Larnder was in command as the orders came through to the *Mackay-Bennett* to stand by to assist in the search for victims. Currently berthed in Halifax, the ship was already busy on the France/Canada communications line, but the ship had some good storage space below which would be utilised for the coffins and corpses that would have to be stowed on board for the journey back to shore.

Within two days of the sinking, the cable ship had embarked 100 tons of ice for the bodies and 100 coffins. Not only that, onboard was Canon Kenneth Hind of Halifax's All Saints Cathedral and John Snow Jr, chief embalmer of the John Snow & Co. undertakers. With the supplies brought on board and the survivors of *Titanic* still out at sea on *Carpathia*, *Mackay-Bennett* sailed in the early afternoon of 17 April 1912 in thick fog, heading out to the disaster zone.

As a result of poor visibility (remember *Carpathia* was heading westbound in this weather), it would take the ship almost four days to get to the reported position of the lost

The cable ship *Mackay-Bennett* in dry dock in Halifax, Nova Scotia. (Notman Studio)

Titanic. The captain instructed all personnel to keep the logs up to date, an order that today means there are detailed records of everything that happened during what must have been a very bleak voyage.

The ship encountered a terrible scene – hundreds of bodies frozen stiff in the cold Atlantic swell. It was immediately obvious that the other ships that were being prepared would have to be brought out to cope with the scale of the task ahead of them. The crew got to work, being careful to show as much respect as possible for each body as it was lifted on board and where possible identified. After just one week they had located 328 bodies and managed to recover 306, of which 116 were buried at sea, the rest of them held on board where space allowed (remember they only had 100 coffins but still almost double that number of corpses). Only fifty-six of these bodies were identified by personal possessions, one of them being the richest man on board, Colonel John Jacob Astor, who had a considerable amount of cash on his person when found.

Other people identified included band leader Wallace Hartley, who was taken back to his hometown of Colne in Lancashire, UK. Strapped to his chest was his violin, engraved with a message from his fiancée Maria. It is interesting that despite being dead, the vast majority of the victims were treated in accordance with the class of ticket that they had purchased – First Class were placed in coffins, Second Class wrapped in canvas and Third Class buried at sea. While it is clear that the victims were treated respectfully by the crew of the cable ship, even in death there was a pecking order.

On 30 April 1912, *Mackay-Bennett* arrived back in Halifax with her tragic cargo where it was unloaded, the jetty crowded with horse and carts taking the coffins away to be buried. With 190 victims to manage, it took some time to unload the corpses in a way that befitted the victims of a disaster that was still very raw just two weeks after it had happened. Those individuals that had been identified were handed back to their families for funeral arrangements. The victims that could not be identified were interred at Fairview Lawn Cemetery with a headstone simply reading 'Died April 15, 1912' and a number beneath. Some of these people were eventually identified, but the rows of identical graves brings home the tragic spectacle that was *Titanic*.

The Astor family offered a substantial reward for whoever recovered the body of Colonel Astor. True to their word, the crew of *Mackay-Bennett* received a large cash sum to split between them. In another sad part of this story, the crew used some of this money to pay for a coffin, headstone and funeral for an unnamed baby that was found and recovered from the scene. For many years, tributes were laid on this grave which simply said, 'Erected to the memory of an unknown child whose remains were recovered after the disaster to the *Titanic* April 15th 1912'. It would be ninety-five years before DNA testing permitted identification of the baby as Sidney Goodwin, a Third Class passenger who perished along with all seven of his family members. When the grave was dug up for the investigation, a small copper plate that read 'Our Babe' was discovered. It had been attached to the coffin, although very little of that or the body now remained.

A total of 121 victims of the *Titanic* disaster were buried at Halifax, an entire section now devoted to this tragic part of the city's history.

Mackay-Bennett had a seamount named after her near the Grand Banks as a tribute to her work during the recovery operation. In 1922, she became a storage hulk in Plymouth Sound and was sunk there in the Second World War during an air raid on the city. *Mackay-Bennett* was eventually salvaged and scrapped in 1965.

The final resting place of *Titanic* victim Sidney Leslie Goodwin. (Chris Meunier)

11

Minia

Type	Cable ship
Length	328.5 feet
Gross tonnage	2,061
Built	London & Glasgow Co., Glasgow
Owners	Anglo American Telegraph Company
Link to *Titanic*	Recovery of victims after disaster

Like *Mackay-Bennett*, the cable ship *Minia* was tasked to recover the *Titanic*'s dead soon after the sinking, although she is rarely mentioned in the annals of *Titanic* history. Resembling a small liner crossed with a luxury yacht, she was built in 1886 to be used for shallow-water cable repairs and maintenance jobs. However, by 1891 she had been fitted out for deeper water work in the Mid-Atlantic area under the charter of the Telegraph Construction and Maintenance Company. After three years working in this field *Minia* was sold to the Anglo-American Telegraph Company.

When the first reports of the *Titanic* disaster started to arrive at wireless stations across the American continent, one of those ships transmitted this information was reportedly the *Minia* off Cape Race saying that the *Titanic* was actually being towed towards the Cape with the purpose of beaching her. This may have been a simple case of it being a mis-heard report as it was so obviously untrue, but this together with the full facts being heard by wireless stations made newspaper editors splash this untruth across their front pages giving false hope to those still awaiting news.

After it became obvious that *Mackay-Bennett* was overwhelmed with the sheer volume of work needed to be carried out following the sinking of *Titanic*, the White Star Line chartered *Minia* to assist with the recovery operation. Under the command of Captain William George Squares deCarteret, she sailed from Halifax on 22 April 1912 and headed out into her usual working area to meet with her counterpart.

On board were embalmer William H. Snow, assistant undertaker and surgeon Will Mosher and the Reverend Henry Ward Cunningham of St George's Church, Halifax, as well as the usual cargo of stores, coffins and embalming fluid. Sailing eastward towards the disaster site, *Minia*'s mission was hampered by bad weather after arriving on scene. As a result, in the course of an entire week on site they only managed to locate and recover seventeen bodies from the *Titanic*, two of whom were buried at sea.

The body of a *Titanic* victim aboard CS *Minia*, 1912. (William J. Parker, carpenter onboard CS *Minia*)

Minia turned for home once again and the fifteen bodies were brought ashore when the vessel came into port on 6 May. After this, she was unloaded and released for her regular duties as a cable ship.

It is estimated that during the thirty-six years *Minia* was in service, she laid around 50,000 nautical miles of cable and undertook repair missions around the globe before she was sold for scrap in 1922. While the story of *Minia* is less well known, in more recent times, some newly discovered items have highlighted her link to *Titanic*.

In 2012, the family of *Minia*'s Second Engineer Francis Tierney appeared in an episode of *History Detectives*, a popular TV documentary series. The programme featured a photo frame that was said to be made of wood retrieved by Tierney from the floating debris where *Titanic* went down. Not only that, photographs of the recovery operation showing the upper deck of *Minia* as the crew were dealing with the dead, a mournful job that you can see etched on their faces, have come to light. Various other small items have appeared on the market that are said to have come from *Titanic* when *Minia* was carrying out recovery operations. The ship's carpenter William Parker worked these pieces of flotsam into mementos of a worldwide tragedy. The results of the investigation by the *History Detectives* proved that the photo frame did come from *Titanic*'s Grand Staircase, much to the delight of the family who vowed never to sell it, and dispelled the rumour surrounding its origins.

12

Montmagny

Type	Lighthouse supply and buoy tender
Length	212.6 feet
Gross tonnage	1,269
Built	Sorel, Quebec
Owners	Government of Canada
Link to *Titanic*	Recovery of victims after disaster

Launched in 1909 at the builder's yard in Sorel, Quebec, the Canadian resupply vessel *Montmagny* is another ship that is barely mentioned but was an integral part of the *Titanic* story in the aftermath of the disaster.

Operated by the Canadian Department of Marine and Fisheries, she was the third ship to be chartered by the White Star Line to hunt for victims of the *Titanic* sinking. After *Minia* had completed her work, *Montmagny* was tasked with taking over. She sailed from Sorel with two captains on board, Peter Crerar Johnson, who was in charge in international waters, and Francois Xavier Pouliot, who was in command in home waters. The latter had recently been in the newspapers when he presided over a court case in Quebec in 1911 concerning the investigation into the sinking of the steamer *General Wolfe* in June of that year after a collision with the *Aranmore* in the St Lawrence River. The master and first officer of *General Wolfe* were found guilty of cowardice after they abandoned ship and in doing so left everybody else still on board. The captain of *Aranmore* was guilty of negligence in the case of the collision itself.

Once again, a recovery team was prepared for the *Montmagny* and they embarked to deal with the expected influx of corpses. St Paul's Church of Halifax sent the Reverend Samuel Prince and St Mary's Basilica despatched Father Patrick McQuillan. The undertaker that had been out on *Mackay-Bennett*, John Snow Jr, was brought on board, as was Cecil Zink of Dartmouth.

As *Minia* came into port on 6 May, *Montmagny* headed out to sea. Once again, bad weather hampered the efforts of the crew and they managed to recover only four bodies, one of whom was buried at sea. This brought the total number of *Titanic* victims recovered by all three ships to 329.

After almost a week at sea the bodies were sent to Louisbourg in Nova Scotia where they were then taken to Halifax by train and *Montmagny* continued her search. However, by now the only thing that remained was random pieces of wreckage dotted about the ocean and spread over a wide area. On 19 May, *Montmagny* met up with a vessel named *Algerine*

Montmagny. (Historic Ships Network)

at sea and then headed back to Halifax, where she arrived four days later to continue her normal duties.

In the early hours of 17 March 1914, *Montmagny* was at Duncan's Cover, Nova Scotia, when the steamship *City of Sydney* broadcast an SOS after going aground at Shag Rock, near Sambro Lighthouse. *Montmagny* and two tugs raced to the scene and were on standby to assist the stricken vessel. *City of Sydney* was a total loss but thankfully everybody was saved by the fleet of ships that went to the scene.

Six months later, almost to the day, *Montmagny* was hit by tragedy herself. On 14 September 1914, at around 0500 hours, she was on a voyage from Quebec to the Strait of Belle Isle with supplies for the lighthouses in the area when she was rammed by the Black Diamond collier *Lingan* off Crane Island in the St Lawrence River. On board were not just the ship's crew but also the families of the lighthouse keepers, as well as coal and various other provisions required to keep the lighthouse operating. In a bank of fog, the ship sank within just a few minutes, with fourteen people killed, eleven of them children. The victims were found to be the Belle Isle lighthouse keeper's wife, Mrs Richard, who was on board with seven children, and the wife of the Flower Island's keeper, Mrs Lavalee, and her four children, all of whom were lost. Second Officer Lachance was last seen trying to save two of the children. The rest of the survivors were picked up by the collier *Potana* and taken to Grosse Isle where the government boat *Alice* headed back to Quebec for them to be taken ashore along with the bodies of two small children.

In 2011, the documentary *In the Wake of Titanic: The CGS Montmagny Story* was broadcast and told the story of the ship and her involvement in the *Titanic* disaster, showing archive documents and a life preserver recovered from the *Titanic* wreckage by one of the crew. Although she had a small role to play in the aftermath of the sinking of *Titanic*, her tragic ending was one that deserves more attention. However, there is no memorial to this disaster.

13

Algerine

Type	Cargo/passenger vessel
Length	172.1 feet
Gross tonnage	505
Built	Harland & Wolff, Belfast
Owners	Bowring Bros Ltd, Newfoundland
Link to *Titanic*	Recovery of victims after disaster

Algerine was the fourth and final ship to be chartered to search for the bodies of victims of the *Titanic* disaster. Built in 1880 at the same shipyard as *Titanic*, she was quite a small vessel considering her passenger-carrying capabilities. She was built for the Royal Navy as a gunboat and served on the West Coast of Africa Station. The lead of three ships of the Algerine class of gun vessel, *Algerine* was commissioned on 3 November 1881 in Sheerness before she was sold to a civilian company in 1892 and converted to a cargo ship, a new *Algerine* being launched in 1895 and going on to have a successful career in China.

In June 1901, *Algerine* was briefly mentioned in the newspapers going to the assistance of the steamer *Assyrian*, which had grounded in fog off the Canadian coast, and she stood by with several tugs. That same month she was close by when SS *Lusitania* was wrecked, also off the Canadian coast (not to be confused with the larger *Lusitania* sunk in 1915 by U-boat).

Used as a seal hunting vessel, in 1907 she was in the headlines once more when she arrived at St John's with only 500 seals on board, not a good catch for a ship of this size. This was because her rudder was broken but also at this time several other sealing vessels were damaged or even had to be abandoned and their crews rescued. Another report two years later stated that *Algerine* had caught 8,000 seals, a much more realistic figure and what might be expected of a ship of this type.

A little is known about the career of this ship and photographs show her to be a steam-powered sailing vessel that could double up as a sealing ship. After three ships had gone out to recover *Titanic* victims it became apparent that by this stage there was no point in sending out larger vessels as the chances of recovering bodies were rapidly diminishing. On 16 May 1912, she sailed from St John's and met *Montmagny* out at sea to hand over the tasking. On board was Captain John Jackman and two undertakers and no religious figure, demonstrating how confident they were of actually finding anything.

However, *Algerine* did find somebody, just one body, that of Saloon Steward James McGrady. He was the final *Titanic* victim to be recovered of a total of 330 after a month and a half of continuous searching. The ship spent three weeks out at sea but found

Algerine. (A 9-42 - The Rooms Provincial Archives)

Algerine. (Maritime History Archive, Canada)

nothing more, the body being taken back to her home port and sent to Halifax on board the steamship *Florizel*. (*Florizel* would be involved in a headline-hitting sinking and rescue herself in 1918 on the Newfoundland coast with the loss of ninety-four lives.)

This was the final attempt at locating victims of *Titanic*, the rest by now having drifted too far away, sunk or been consumed by the sea. Many hundreds more went down with the ship, their boots laying side by side, the only evidence of them ever being there and would not be seen again for over seventy years.

Ironically, *Algerine* suffered a similar fate to *Titanic* just three months later on 16 July 1912. During a voyage in ballast from the Hudson Bay to St John's she became trapped in ice and crushed at Ponds Inlet, Baffin Island, and sank. Her crew were rescued by the steamship *Neptune* and taken to St John's in Newfoundland where they were landed on 15 September, two months after she had gone down.

14

Mount Temple

Type	Passenger/cargo liner
Length	485 feet
Gross tonnage	8,790 (at the time of *Titanic* sinking)
Built	Armstrong Whitworth & Co., Newcastle
Owners	Canadian Pacific Railway
Link to *Titanic*	Response to distress call

Launched on 18 June 1901, the liner *Mount Temple* was built for the Elder Dempster & Company fleet to fulfil its role as a large ship that could carry both passengers and cargo, not one that would break any speed records but it would do the job required to a good standard. Her upper deck consisted of four large masts and one single funnel, her name in white on the dark hull down the side of her bows. She made her maiden voyage out of the River Tyne just three months later on 18 September and arrived on the other side of the Atlantic into the American port of New Orleans on 9 October, a journey of three weeks.

Mount Temple had the ability to carry 1,250 passengers in Third Class along with just 14 others in Cabin Class as well as a crew of 117. Before the end of the year, however, she was assigned to the Admiralty and used as a transport ship between New Orleans and Durban, assisting in the Boer War in the South African region. Her service to her country ending in May 1902 by which time she had delivered over 3,000 horses and thousands of tons of supplies to troops.

On 24 February 1903, *Mount Temple* was out at sea when word was received that Canadian Pacific Railway had taken over fourteen of Elder Dempster's ships for an agreed price. *Mount Temple* was brought into port and refitted to her new owner's specifications before once again heading out to sea, this time on the Liverpool to Montreal route under her different owners.

On 20 November 1907, the ship sailed from Antwerp, Belgium, with 633 passengers on board and around 150 crew members for a routine journey that would end in Saint John, New Brunswick. As the ship approached the Canadian coast on 1 December, the weather was getting progressively worse, the visibility reducing and the snow making the driving of the ship ever more difficult. At 0244 hours the following morning, while believing that the lights they were currently seeing were that of another ship passing close by, *Mount Temple* ran aground at West Ironbound Island, off the coast of Nova Scotia. The ship was well and truly stranded, the rocks piercing the hull and the continuous waves smashing into the lifeboats, destroying many of them and leaving the passengers and crew with less and

Mount Temple aground, 1907. (Unknown)

less chance of survival. A huge rescue operation was launched after distress signals were picked up and before long the hundreds of *Mount Temple* passengers were being rescued by clinging on to a basket that would take them from the stranded ship up the nearby cliffs via a long cable. By the early evening of 3 December, the evacuation had been successful and everybody had been saved. This was a huge triumph for those taking part, let alone the grateful faces of the survivors who were now free of the shipwreck.

It would be a while before *Mount Temple* was back at sea, but she was still salvageable, although the chances of recovering her were slight. After several months of being stuck, the ship was eventually pulled off the rocks on 15 April 1908 and even managed to sail under her own power to the nearby port of Lunenburg. By the end of August 1908, all repairs had been carried out at considerable cost to the owners and by September she was back at sea again.

However, this was not the end of *Mount Temple*'s mishaps. Just a few years later, on 14 October 1911, she was in collision with the steamer *Osterley* at anchor at Tilbury Dock as *Mount Temple* was navigating to enter Gravesend port. She sustained slight damage to the bow but nothing too serious. On 18 January 1912, *Mount Temple* located the steamer *Dart* in the Mid-Atlantic, the ship drifting with a damaged rudder, and stood by her in case help was needed. Assistance was not required and so she went on her way the following day.

On the journey that would make her famous, *Mount Temple* sailed from Antwerp on 3 April 1912 under the command of James Henry Moore. Moore was overseeing a crew of 143 as well as a complement of 1,466 passengers for the passage to Saint John and there was no reason to believe this voyage would be any different to the others, save for the amount of ice that was in the area. It was around eleven minutes past midnight on 15 April when wireless operator John Durrant was about to go to bed for the night but stopped in his tracks when he heard something that shocked him. *Titanic* was sinking after an iceberg collision, the position given being wrong at the time (although as is now known all the positions were wrong and were nowhere near where the wreck of *Titanic* was found). He acknowledged the message, and a steward took it up to the bridge as quickly as possible.

The captain was woken up and he knew that while procedure dictated he must avoid ice, a distress message of this magnitude meant speed was critical with the number of lives at stake. He ordered the ship to turn around and head towards *Titanic*'s position as fast as possible, the position of *Titanic* known today meaning *Mount Temple* was around 61 miles away.

The rest of the crew were roused from their beds, preparations were made to receive a large number of survivors and the lifeboats were uncovered to commence transfer of any personnel. Unfortunately, the vast amount of ice meant that the ship was forced to slow down to navigate around it, keeping in mind that the dark night and the inability to see ice is what made *Titanic* hit the berg in the first place. *Mount Temple* reached the position that *Titanic* later confirmed was correct at 41. 46N 50. 14W but found nothing – no wreckage, no survivors, no evidence of a huge shipwreck. The officers and lookouts on watch scanned the sea for any trace of *Titanic* but could see nothing amiss.

As the morning wore on the other rescue ships were seen in the area, *Carpathia* and *Californian* by now combing the sea in the hope of finding some people still alive. By 0926 hours *Carpathia* reported that all twenty lifeboats had been located and that there was no need to carry on searching. *Mount Temple* was now able to continue her voyage and re-store all her life-saving equipment.

When the ship reached her port, the controversy started as several passengers and crew were overheard talking openly about the ship being close to *Titanic* during the sinking, some even witnessing the rockets and the ship sinking but nothing was done to help. Some even suggested that the ship got within 5 miles of *Titanic* and was indeed the mystery ship that was talked about later as being between *Titanic* and *Californian*. This was not brought up at either inquiry and further investigations by historians over the years have shown that it was not possible for *Mount Temple* to have reached *Titanic*'s position any quicker than she did. To mark her role in the attempted rescue, Mount Temple Seamount on the Grand Banks was named after her.

Mount Temple was involved in another mishap when she grounded on 24 September 1913 soon after leaving Montreal bound for London and Antwerp. It took two days to release her from the mud and take her to Montreal for repairs. A year later, on the outbreak of the First World War, the ship was once again requisitioned for transportation of troops and cargo between Britain and France, a gun being mounted on her stern for protection against enemy vessels and submarines.

In August 1915, there was another ownership change when Canadian Pacific and Allan Line merged to form Canadian Pacific Ocean Services Ltd. Two months later *Mount Temple* was released back to her civilian owners to resume normal services under her new ownership. She did, however, transport 1,200 German prisoners of war from France to Britain after the Battle of Loos soon after, but it was not long before the ship was undertaking journeys to and from Canada once again.

Under the command of Captain Alfred Henry Sargent, *Mount Temple* sailed from Montreal on 3 December 1916 with a crew of 109, a general cargo and over 700 horses.

Mount Temple in the Thames. (Unknown)

Among the cargo on board were twenty-two crates containing the fossils of dinosaurs bound for the British Museum in London. These were excavated in Alberta from what is now known as the Dinosaur Provincial Park, a UNESCO World Heritage Site.

The ship's first port of call was Brest on the French coast before she would continue on to Liverpool. However, just three days after setting sail she encountered the German merchant raider *Möwe* which chased *Mount Temple* until being forced to stop by shooting her gun across the bow.

Incredibly, the crew of *Mount Temple* fought back with the ship's 3-inch gun, but *Möwe* hit back harder and blasted the gun crews as well as the upper deck, killing three crew, a fourth succumbing to injuries later. The ship was forced to surrender and the people on board were taken off before explosives were then rigged to detonate the ship that evening. At 1800 hours on 6 December 1916, *Mount Temple* exploded and sank around 620 nautical miles off Fastnet.

Mount Temple's occupants were transferred to Germany to be interred in a prisoner of war camp. Any American citizens were sent back to their homeland as their country was neutral in the war at this point. *Möwe* sank forty-one ships in her career through raids or mine laying, but was herself later sunk in the Second World War in an air raid on a Norwegian fjord.

Today, the conspiracy surrounding the role of *Mount Temple* during the sinking of *Titanic*, as well as that of *Californian*, still rears its head from time to time. Documentaries have been made and books published about this scenario, but the only thing that is ever uncovered is that Captain Moore put his ship at risk in order to get there as quickly as possible, despite not being able to rescue a single soul. Although the outcome was disheartening, the crew were still heroes that night and the name of their ship is forever associated with the most famous shipwreck in history.

Mount Temple remains undiscovered and is thought to be sitting at a depth of 4,725 metres. No serious searches for the wreck have ever taken place. She holds one unique record, that of being of the only recorded ship to have been lost at sea with dinosaurs on board.

15

La Touraine

Type	Ocean liner
Length	520 feet, 2 inches
Gross tonnage	8,429
Built	Cantiers de Penhoet, St Nazaire, France
Owners	French Line
Link to *Titanic*	One of the ships that transmitted ice warnings to *Titanic*

Launched on 21 March 1890, the liner *La Touraine* was constructed for the Le Havre to New York service to meet the ever-increasing passenger demand that French Line was fast becoming an expert in. With triple expansion engines and twin screws, she could go at 19 knots, her black hull sporting two tall masts with two black funnels in the middle. She could accommodate over 1,000 passengers in three classes (392 in First, 98 in Second and 600 in Third Class) in addition to her crew.

On her maiden voyage on 20 June 1891 her speed enabled a crossing time of six days, seventeen hours and thirty minutes. A year later, she got her speed up to a record 21.2 knots over a measured mile, although no award was won for this and the coveted Blue Riband remained just out of reach on a number of occasions.

On 21 January 1903, fire damaged the ship while she was berthed in her home port of Le Havre. The flames spread to the First Class Dining Room and Grand Staircase as well as several of her de luxe cabins, all of which had to be rebuilt. The repairs were successfully carried out and *La Touraine* was soon back at sea even if it was at a reduced capacity, her recent refit having lowered her First and Second Class passenger-carrying capacity but instead increased her capacity for Third Class.

On 12 April 1912, she was in the Mid-Atlantic trying to avoid ice like every other vessel and transmitted a number of ice warnings to nearby ships, among them *Titanic*. With no further issues during that voyage, she continued onwards, hearing about the disaster long after it had taken place. Although she had been one of the ships to transmit the warnings in the first place, *La Touraine* is very rarely mentioned in this context.

By May 1913, she was only carrying Second and Third Class passengers on her Le Havre to Montreal route. In October of that year, on this route she was one of the ships that came to the aid of the burning liner *Volturno*, although she almost became a casualty herself when coming within just 15 feet of colliding with the Red Star Line vessel *Kroonland*. With so many ships there to assist there was very little that *La Touraine* could do.

Left: A postcard featuring *La Touraine*.

Below: Another postcard featuring *La Touraine*.

When the First World War broke out the French government took over many liners and tasked them with a variety of roles, and *La Touraine* found herself being used for wartime work like many others. Following the war, passenger services were a lot less prominent, and the ship was sold in 1922 after her final voyage had ended. In October 1923, she was taken to Dunkirk where she was finally scrapped.

16

Lapland

Type	Ocean liner
Length	605.8 feet
Gross tonnage	17,540 (at the time of *Titanic* sinking)
Built	Harland & Wolff, Belfast
Owners	Red Star Line
Link to *Titanic*	Returning survivors to UK

The Red Star liner *Lapland* had a very small role in the *Titanic* story but it was one that made the headlines at the time along with a considerable number of press photographs – she brought back to Britain a number of the survivors who wanted to return home straight away. Although she was Belfast-built, she was owned by a Belgian company and launched on 27 June 1908, commencing her maiden voyage on 10 April 1909 (three years to the day before *Titanic*). She had two funnels and four masts, her route taking her between Antwerp, Dover and New York on a weekly trip for up to 1,500 passengers at a speed of around 17 knots. That year she made the news a few times as several liners found themselves racing each other to be the first across the Atlantic, the excitement on board something to write home about as each ship made every effort to be the winner of that crossing.

In September 1911, a bizarre incident at sea involved a Christian sect that was travelling in a schooner named *Coronet*. On board were several dozen followers and their leader 'Reverend' Frank Sandford. Randomly travelling around the world on the sailing vessel, by this point the occupants did not have enough food to survive and so sent out a distress signal. This was picked up by *Lapland* on 29 September, the message simply saying, 'We are starving.' The liner came close to the *Coronet* and a boat was sent over to the grateful passengers loaded with supplies to keep them from starving to death on the high seas. *Lapland* continued her journey but hitting rough weather not long after the interaction *Coronet* had many fear that further distress signals heard meant that the schooner had gone down with no survivors. As it happened, *Coronet* had survived the storm, although six passengers later died of scurvy on board and Sandford was jailed for their deaths upon his return to the US.

Lapland didn't make real headlines until 1912 when White Star Line was obliged to hire her to bring a total of 167 *Titanic* survivors back to Britain after they had been held in the US to testify at the inquiry or assist the investigators, others remaining behind. Also on board were 1,927 bags of mail that should have been loaded on to *Titanic* upon her departure from New York. Lapland sailed on 20 April, many of those left behind looking on having hopes of being placed aboard the ship at the last minute, in some cases these

A postcard featuring *Lapland*.

being crew members who were now destitute as all their belongings had gone down with the ship and their pay having stopped the moment the liner sank.

For those who did make it on *Lapland*, they were anything but lucky. Escorted on board, many of them chose to remain silent, although some may have been coerced into remaining tight-lipped. Later news reports suggest that those who had come from the lost liner were more or less kept in isolation for the whole voyage, although the ship made the crossing in good time, arriving off Plymouth on 28 April. Approaching the coast and heading slowly through Plymouth Sound past Drake Island, the warship HMS *Theseus* was at anchor nearby as the ship moved around carefully to her berth, much to the delight of the families who had been waiting on the Hoe for many hours. As soon as the ship came into the Sound some of *Titanic*'s crew were taken straight from the ship onto tugs, although many others were detained by the Board of Trade in order to get written depositions regarding their experiences on *Titanic*. These interviews could not take place until the British Seafarers Union representatives were also present, the tender *Sir Richard Grenville* transferring personnel to and from the ship which was now at anchor in Plymouth Sound near *Theseus*.

The crew were taken to a waiting room at the Great Western Docks to be interviewed, their story meticulously recorded by officials. Once this was done, they were put on a train to Southampton accompanied by the cheers of the crowds waiting at the dockyard gates. The press was told that the survivors were not detained against their will but were 'invited' to remain behind until spoken to by officials.

Lapland soon resumed her normal routine with regular runs across the Atlantic, transporting passengers like US golf champion Francis Ouimet on his way to take part in the British championships in spring 1914. What made this voyage special was that the captain allowed nets to be rigged so the young sportsman could practise while at sea, a gesture that he greatly appreciated. The year after there was a minor scandal when US immigration laws once again came under scrutiny for being too harsh, leading to a man being detained on board the ship despite him having onward travel to Canada and having no intention of staying in the US. He was made to stay on board *Lapland* overnight for fear he may head straight to one of the poor houses as he suffered with sciatic rheumatism. What they failed to take into account was this particular man, W. A. Anderson, was one of the richest men in Canada, leading to embarrassment on the part of the immigration officials who failed to listen to reason.

When war broke out in 1914, *Lapland* was taken to Britain after Antwerp fell into German hands, the ship resuming passenger services under new UK ownership. On 15 September 1915, two bottles containing what was described as 'high explosives' were found on board as the ship was about to sail from New York to Liverpool. This news was covered in the newspapers but what happened subsequently was not reported and the ship carried on with her journey.

War was soon to catch up with *Lapland* and on 7 April 1917 she was off the *Mersey Bar Lightship* when she hit a mine laid by submarine *UC-65*. This caused damage to the hull but thankfully she did not sink. However twenty-five-year-old trimmer James O'Connor was killed by the shock, his name now listed on the Merchant Navy memorial at Tower Hill. The ship was able to limp back to Liverpool where repairs were carried out. During the rest of the war, she was used to carry troops on several occasions across to the war zones.

The Armistice, and the end of the war, was declared on 11 November 1918 when *Lapland* had been out at sea for three days with over 1,000 passengers, heading to Southampton. She came to a point in the Mid-Atlantic where Captain Bradshaw ordered the engines stopped at the request of the king. A two-minute silence was observed and one of the passengers, Bishop Burt, gave an address to those attending the ceremony while the national anthems of Britain and the Allied nations were sung. Following this, £200 was collected for charity after an appeal was made by General Sir Anthony Bowlby on behalf of St Dunstan's Hospital for the Blind. Before long *Lapland*'s engines were back up and running and the ship was once again making headway east towards Southampton, where she arrived a week later.

After the war, *Lapland* was taken over by White Star Line and commenced the Southampton to New York routes, starting with taking soldiers who had been fighting in the war back to the US. She was soon back to entertaining the celebrities of the day such as Mary Pickford and her husband Douglas Fairbanks as they travelled on their honeymoon to Europe. The so-called 'King and Queen of Hollywood' attracted a lot of press attention on this particular trip and would continue to do so for a long time after *Lapland* arrived in Southampton eight days later to a crowd of adoring fans eager to glimpse the golden couple who had hitherto only been seen in black-and-white films. Another event that caused a press presence in 1924 was the landing of twenty Canadians competing in the Wembley Rodeo at the newly built stadium of that name in London. Photographers snapped a group of people wearing cowboy outfits marching down the upper deck of the *Lapland* with names like 'Skeets' Bill and 'Bonnie' McCarroll.

Lapland's voyages were usually uneventful, but one particular journey in January 1923 was noteworthy when in the space of five days the ship received distress calls from five different ships that required assistance the in Mid-Atlantic. Due to the distance and the fact that other ships were closer and managed to get there first, *Lapland* was unable to assist any of these vessels. In July, there was yet another immigration issue involving the ship when a baby was born to Polish parents on board *Lapland*. As the ship was flying a British flag the nationality of that baby was officially British according to immigration officials in New York, despite the nationality of the parents. The fact that the British immigration quota had been exhausted by July meant that the baby was held at Ellis Island until a solution was found. In the meantime, the mother and two other children had to remain with the baby while the husband went Pennsylvania and awaited his family's arrival.

On 11 January 1924, *Lapland* found herself in distress while alongside New York preparing to depart on a Mediterranean cruise when a fire broke out on board. The cause was not officially known but it was believed to have originated among some old bales of rope and then spread until the alarm was eventually raised and fire boats heading to the burning ship. The firefighting teams tackled the blaze and got it under control by 1500 hours that afternoon. Incredibly, the fire did not really affect the ship, although some cargo was found to be damaged when the ship was inspected further.

The year didn't end well *Lapland* as she was involved in an incident that was as unbelievable as it was rare. On 16 December, she was heading into the Belgian port of Antwerp when she collided with the British steamship *Eston* and the Danish vessel *Java*, causing serious damage to the Danish ship. While *Lapland* sustained some minor damage, *Eston* was fine, but then *Eston* accidentally collided with the nearby German steamship *Helios* and incredibly still remained undamaged.

The 1920s ticked by but drama was never far away. Aviators James DeWitt Hill and Lloyd Bertaud planned to fly non-stop from the US to Rome in the aircraft 'Old Glory'. They were accompanied by *New York Daily Mirror* editor Phillip Payne who was to report on this feat of endurance. Departing from Maine on 6 September 1927, the aircraft headed east and reported its position without issues. However, by the early hours of 7 September, they had encountered bad weather and sent out distress signals, *Lapland* being one of five liners to speed to the nearest point in the vicinity of the lost aircraft. Sadly, nothing was heard from the aviators again and the plane's wreckage was found days later.

Another chapter in the life of this ship was written in November the same year when Second Electrician Florent Lamot was arrested. He was thought to have disproportionately large feet until it was discovered he was actually smuggling £20,000 of diamonds in his shoes as part of an organised crime gang. He had done this several times on a number of voyages until somebody got wise and had him watched when he left the ship.

In the early 1930s, *Lapland* took on a new role as a cruise ship to the Mediterranean, her passengers enjoying holiday destinations like Gibraltar, Algiers and Barcelona. The time spent at sea was a delight for those on board, where sunbathers could wear the fashion of the day on deck or just soak up the sun's rays, play deck sports or take part in events such as the farewell gala on the night before returning home. The most popular activities were using the swimming pool and the cinema where 'talking pictures' could be enjoyed, something that was unheard of when the ship was launched. At this point in the twentieth century the cruise liner was a very new concept and the few ships that were used in this capacity would send updates to the newspapers, which eagerly reported on the antics, port visits, entertainment and comments by the passengers. Excursions were laid on for those who wanted to explore the ports, or they could go off themselves if they so wanted, a wander around the Rock of Gibraltar being quite popular with the 600-plus tourists.

Lapland was due to have an overhaul in October 1933 and her owners, by now F. Leyland and Co. Ltd, decided that the cost of this would not be beneficial. The worldwide Depression and the decrease in both holidays and the North Atlantic trade soon put paid to the story of *Lapland*. On 25 October, it was officially reported that she would make one last voyage and that would be to the scrapyard. In less than five months she had steamed 28,000 miles to almost fifty ports, carrying 5,000 passengers over the summer. She was sold to Japanese scrap merchants for around £29,650, a very high figure paid for a merchant ship for scrapping, ending her days broken up in Osaka in 1934.

17

Nomadic

Type	Tender
Length	220 feet
Gross tonnage	1,260
Built	Harland & Wolff, Belfast
Owners	White Star Line
Link to *Titanic*	Ferried passengers and mail during Cherbourg stop

After the decision had been made to build three monstrous ships, White Star Line commissioned the same builders to construct two small vessels that would be tasked to ferry the people, luggage and mail out to the ship while it was at anchor in the French port of Cherbourg. Designed by Thomas Andrews (who would lose his life on *Titanic* in the sinking), *Nomadic* was launched on 25 April 1911 and completed on 27 May just in time for *Olympic*'s maiden voyage just over two weeks later.

Nomadic arrived in Cherbourg to begin her tendering career on 3 June and once *Olympic* sailed from Southampton on 14 June she was all ready to begin her first job with the new liner. The size of *Olympic* compared with that of the jetties and the harbour itself meant that the liner would anchor inside the breakwater. Once the passengers had completed all the relevant checks at the terminal, they were allowed onto *Nomadic* to begin the journey out to the middle of the harbour, no doubt filled with excitement at being able to board the newest tender to go out to the newest and biggest ship.

On board, *Nomadic* had been fitted out so that the passengers boarding her would already think that the high standards of White Star had been met. This was evidenced by the wood panelling, elegant stairways and ability to see through the windows while enjoying the time sat taking in the surroundings as the tender gently rocked to the motion of the harbour waters.

On reaching the ship, a gangway was rigged at the accommodation entrance so that passengers would experience as little disruption as possible while being transferred from *Nomadic* onto the liner. Once all the baggage, supplies and mail had been sent up, *Nomadic* would cast off and return to her jetty ready for the next voyage.

On 10 April 1912, *Titanic*'s maiden voyage began with sailing from Southampton, arriving at Cherbourg in the early evening where *Nomadic* was ready to transfer everyone on board. Arriving on the liner's starboard side, she embarked onto the huge liner a total of 172 passengers, including millionaire John Jacob Astor, the Duff-Gordons and Margaret 'the Unsinkable Molly' Brown to name but a few. Many of these passengers were on a

A postcard featuring *Nomadic*.

trip across Europe, taking in the sights and sounds, although for Astor it was a chance to get away from the publicity surrounding his marriage to the pregnant eighteen-year-old Madeleine who was accompanying him. When *Titanic* sank, *Nomadic* was left with just one White Star liner to tend to and although she was used for other ships in the meantime, it would be some time before larger ships appeared in any great numbers.

However, as with many ships of this era, just two years later *Nomadic* was in a new wartime role. She was taken over by the French government to be used as a minesweeper and, later in the war, to transport American troops to the port of Brest. Although she eventually returned to her normal duties, by the mid-1930s White Star Line was in difficulties and *Nomadic* was sold to a French company known as the Société Cherbourgeoise de Sauvetage et de Remorquage (Cherbourg Tow and Rescue Society). In 1934, she was renamed *Ingenieur Minard*, her tender days now over following the redevelopment of Cherbourg meaning ships could now go alongside a jetty instead of anchoring.

It was over two decades since her wartime service, but upon the invasion of France in 1940 the vessel resumed her previous role. When the evacuation of Cherbourg was ordered the *Ingenieur Minard* sped to Britain, where she was requisitioned by the Royal Navy as an accommodation vessel in Portsmouth.

While the port of Cherbourg took a battering, it was clear that the Nazis were at last being beaten back and that tendering might once again be an option for the plucky ship. She headed back across the Channel and carried on what she knew best, this time tending the liners *Queen Mary* and *Queen Elizabeth* which were some of the largest ships in the world at this time, bigger even than the ships she was originally designed to meet.

In 1968, the future of the ocean liner was in peril as the jet airplane made long Atlantic crossings obsolete. *Ingenieur Minard* was retired from service and in 1969 was taken to Le Havre. Five years later she was saved from the scrapyard by Yvon Vincent who had visions of turning the former tender into a floating restaurant on the River Seine in Paris, in view of the Eiffel Tower, with her name on her bow once again reading *Nomadic*.

Twenty years later, the business collapsed and *Nomadic* lay alongside her berth on the Seine empty and derelict, eventually being seized by the authorities in 2002 and towed back to Le Havre. When Vincent died in 2005 it was revealed that a buyer was needed for *Nomadic* otherwise she would be scrapped. Alarmed that this piece of history would be turned to razor blades, enthusiasts, historians and experts got together to save the *Nomadic*. Fundraising and publicity events gained support from around the world, the Department for Social Development in Northern Ireland purchasing *Nomadic* in 2006 for €1 above the reserve price. With the vessel now under new ownership, work began to bring her back to Belfast for restoration.

After a lot of hard work and dedication, she was carefully placed onto a barge and brought out of French waters for the first time since the war. She slowly made her way up the Irish Sea and finally arrived in Belfast, the city of her birth, on 12 July 2006 to the delights of the crowds that now welcomed her. The last White Star Line vessel was now home for good.

After a long process that is still ongoing at the time of writing, *Nomadic* was placed in the Hamilton Graving Dock. She was eventually opened to visitors in 2013, over a year after

Nomadic in Paris, May 2000. (Author)

the centenary of *Titanic*'s sinking but in sight of the huge new Titanic Belfast museum that has come to symbolise the shipbuilding and history of this city. She sports the original White Star Line colours with a black hull and, although her rigging is missing, her single yellow and black funnel is now looking as good as new, the same way *Titanic*'s passengers saw her over a century ago as they boarded for their final fateful journey.

Thanks to the people who care for this vessel, *Nomadic*'s story will live on.

Author's note: In May 2000 I took a trip to Paris to see *Nomadic*. Painted white, she looked badly in need of restoration and appeared to have been derelict for quite a while. The entranceway was close enough for me to jump on board and have my photograph taken. After taking photographs of her from every angle, I went away hoping that someday she would be restored.

In February 2020, my family and I went to Belfast and I saw *Nomadic* once again, now restored to her former glory. I had my photograph taken in the exact same place, but this time she was open for visitors and I could finally see the magnificence of this historic vessel. The information boards and audio/visual references tell the story of the ship and her wartime exploits, proving that she was more than just a part of *Titanic*'s story and a ship in her own right.

Nomadic in Belfast, February 2020. (Author)

18

Traffic

Type	Tender
Length	186 feet
Gross tonnage	640
Built	Harland & Wolff, Belfast
Owners	White Star Line
Link to *Titanic*	Built as a tender for Olympic class ships

While *Traffic* was built with *Nomadic* to tender to the two liners, she was smaller than her running mate. On 27 April 1911, she was launched, two days after *Nomadic* took to the water, the same going for their sea trials, *Traffic* completing hers two days after *Nomadic* on 19 May. They were handed over to their owners on 27 May, ready to start work at their new home port in France.

During the preparation of the *Olympic* both *Nomadic* and *Traffic* escorted the liner down to Southampton on 31 May 1911. The two tenders then broke away to continue on their own journey to Cherbourg to be ready for the liner's maiden voyage port visit there in just a few days' time. Right on time, *Olympic* arrived in Cherbourg and went to anchor behind the breakwater. *Traffic* was there loaded up and ready to take the Third Class passengers out from the jetty to the ship.

This was the same job she would do on 10 April 1912 when *Titanic* made her stop there that evening. A total of 102 Third-Class passengers would depart *Traffic* and board the *Titanic* for her passage to destiny. On board there were also a number of cases of French wine, bottled water, champagne, beer and numerous bags of mail for the voyage. Edging up to the liner on her port side, *Traffic* took up her position while her sister ship *Nomadic* was on the starboard side, although *Traffic* actually got to *Titanic* first.

As the First World War impacted France more than any other country, the two tenders had to remain where they were. *Traffic* took on American troops in 1917 and would continue to ferry them until 1919, a year after the war had ended. By then, she had returned to normal service with White Star Line until, like *Nomadic*, she was sold off to carry on the same job under the new owners, Compagnie Cherbourgeoise de Transbordement.

On 5 June 1929, the tender collided with the White Star Liner *Homeric*, not a bad accident but enough for her to be refitted with new propellers in order for the crew to be able to handle her better. This did not prevent another collision on 9 December with the *Minnewaska* of the American Transport Line, again the damage being only slight.

Left and below: Traffic.
(Philippe Delaunoy)

When the two tenders were sold again in 1934, this time to Société Cherbourgeoise de Sauvetage et de Remorquage, *Traffic* was renamed *Ingenieur Riebell* with the registration number X23. Upon the outbreak of the Second World War, it was clear that France was going to fall and on 17 June 1940 the ship was scuttled by the French military to prevent the Germans being able to use both the ship and the port. However, shortly afterwards the invaders raised the tender and within months she was being used as a convoy escort vessel, although her story came to an abrupt end on 17 January 1941. While carrying out convoy duties and coastal patrols, *Ingenieur Riebell* was torpedoed and sunk in the English Channel.

Despite claims that she was salvaged, there is nothing concrete to say that the former *Titanic*'s tender was ever seen again, and her wreck location remains unknown. What made it even more sad was that several people who had worked on both tenders witnessed her demise.

19

Caronia

Type	Ocean liner
Length	678 feet
Gross tonnage	19,594
Built	John Brown & Co., Clydebank
Owners	Cunard Line
Link to *Titanic*	Transmitted ice warnings on night of disaster

Launched on 13 July 1904 by the wife of the US Ambassador, a speech by her husband highlighted the American and British flags flying on the unfinished liner stating that these flags would 'never be further apart' as the friendship between the USA and Cunard was toasted. At the time, this ship was the largest vessel ever launched from an English or Scottish shipyard, so even as her name was announced *Caronia* was breaking records, although this record would be broken on a number of occasions over the coming years. *Caronia* had two tall funnels and could carry 1,550 passengers in three classes (300 in First, 350 in Second and 900 in Third). Her maiden voyage began on 25 February the following year from Liverpool to New York and just a month later the press was labelling the ship practically unsinkable', conveniently missing off the word 'practically' in the headline. This would be famously repeated with the *Titanic* in 1911/1912 and created the myth that ships with these watertight doors fitted were in fact unable to sink. This in turn led to an overconfidence about the ship when it came to evacuation on the night *Titanic* went down.

Caronia took on the role of cruise ship to the Mediterranean in 1906 and as this was before the launching of *Lusitania* and *Mauritania*'s careers, *Caronia* and her sister ship *Carmania* were actually the largest ships in the Cunard fleet at this point. It was using these two ships and the lessons learning on the state of the different engines that it was decided that the future two larger Cunarders would be built with turbine engines instead.

On 16 May 1905, during her third voyage, *Caronia* ran aground off Sandy Hook, this place becoming an accident hotspot for liners, due to dense fog. The pilot on board had to choose between hitting another liner at anchor or ramming a schooner and instead decided to divert off course which resulted in going aground on the sandbank. A number of tugs were sent to the scene, and with the new powerful engines on board *Caronia* was soon back afloat and on her way after forty hours lodged on the sandbank.

On 7 August 1908, she was two days into another voyage from Liverpool to New York when she came upon the barque *Lyderhorn*, a British vessel that was on a voyage from Peru to Rotterdam. *Lyderhorn* had been at sea for 134 days and had completely run out of food, the crew starving for two days. Like *Lapland*, *Caronia* sent over provisions from their own store so that those on board *Lyderhorn* would be able to eat, a drama that seemed to excite *Caronia*'s passengers as news of the incident spread throughout the ship.

A year after this incident, on 14 August 1909, *Caronia* was alongside Liverpool when another nearby Cunard liner, *Lucania*, caught fire. The fire soon spread, the liner burning into the night before sinking at the dockside. Some of the firemen who fell overboard in the sinking had to grasp onto *Caronia*'s hawsers in a bid to survive.

As per her usual Mid-Atlantic crossing, *Caronia* left New York bound for Liverpool on 10 April 1912, under the command of Captain James Barr. Over the coming days *Caronia* found herself in the vicinity of the radio messages that were being transmitted between the ships that were continuously sighting ice as the temperatures in the Mid-Atlantic area plummeted. On the morning of 14 April, *Caronia* transmitted a wireless message warning of ice which was picked up by *Titanic*: 'West-bound steamers report bergs, growlers and field ice in 42 N. from 49 to 51 W.' This message was the same one that had been sent by *Noordam* earlier. At 0944 hours the reply came back from *Titanic*: 'Thanks for message and information. Have had variable weather throughout - Smith.'

That night when disaster struck the distress calls were picked up by *Caronia*, which was around 240 miles away. As *Titanic* was sinking, the Cunarder relayed news of the disaster to SS *Baltic* at around 0030 hours and again at 0053 hours.

Captain Barr testified at the British inquiry into the loss of *Titanic*, stating that this ice warning had not only been transmitted but that *Titanic* had confirmed receipt of it. His evidence was given in the testimony on Day 10 of the inquiry in London's Drill Hall on 17 May 1912.

A postcard featuring *Caronia*. (Author)

In December of that year, a rather different news article about the ship appeared. On one voyage the usual gambling on board involving card players was replaced with the dressing of 250 dolls. These were later distributed to poor children in London. They were a small number of what would eventually total 100,000 dolls dressed up and displayed as part of an *Evening News* promotion about the greatest ever doll show near Westminster Abbey.

There was a small incident involving *Caronia* in the run-up to Christmas. On 23 December, transiting the River Mersey, *Caronia* collided with the smaller Glasgow steamer *Gorilla*, which sustained a small amount of damage. The collision was in fact so slight that most of the passengers on the liner were unaware of anything untoward happening.

The outbreak of war saw *Caronia* transformed into an Armed Merchant Cruiser by the Admiralty, her decks, superstructure and funnel now taking on a dull grey paintwork as she assumed wartime duties. She shone in this phase of her career when, on 19 August 1914, she captured *Odessa*, a German cargo ship full of nitrate, and took her to Berehaven, Ireland. Two months later, on 18 October 1914, she entered Halifax escorting *Brindilla*, believed to be an American oil tanker that had been captured at sea on 13 October by HMS *Suffolk*. It was quickly determined that she was not American but in fact German. Reports stated that the crew members attempted to open the seacocks and flood the ship, and so *Caronia* was obliged to put a further team of people on board. The tanker seemed to have had its name changed from that of *Washington* and it was suspected it was flying the American flag in order to carry contraband across the ocean for German cruisers out at sea. However, the presence of the American flag led to protests in the US at the seizing of an American ship by the British, and eventually Canada was forced to release the vessel after almost two weeks

Another postcard featuring *Caronia*. (Author)

in port to continue her voyage. This was not the end of the issue for *Brindilla*, though, as she continued to be arrested by other ships well into the following year.

Once again, *Caronia* was slightly damaged on 14 April 1915 (the third anniversary of the *Titanic* disaster) when she collided with the schooner *Edward B. Winslow*, although thankfully this did not interrupt her war service. In between these voyages the ship did regular patrols off the east coast of the US before she became a troop transport ship. She continued in this role for the remainder of the conflict, being handed back to Cunard after the war and resuming her normal role after a refit.

At the end of September 1921, *Caronia* was involved in two tragedies in just over a week. On 25 September, as the liner left New York bound for Liverpool, she collided with the sloop *John Anton* and cut the vessel in two. It seemed that the motor of the sloop had stopped at the exact moment that it was crossing the bows of the liner and *Caronia* sliced straight through her, the smaller boat sinking immediately and killing all three crew on board. *Caronia* proceeded to anchor while a search operation was carried out and damage to the liner was assessed before proceeding onwards around an hour later. However, the remaining journey was not without incident as two days later a fifty-nine-year-old passenger travelling alone, Judge Peter Stenger Grosscup, was taken ill and died suddenly of heart failure. His body was taken back to the US, and he was buried in Ohio.

In August 1922, the press was watching *Caronia* as she left Cuxhaven in Germany bound for Southampton with a man named Gerard Lee Bevan on board. He was wanted for fraud with regards to a huge investment failure and was being brought back to London to face the music. This was the era of prohibition in the US and the complete ban on alcohol also applied to ships entering American ports. Ships were likely to be searched for contraband booze and in some cases their own stores had to be depleted before entering American ports. One declaration stated that 'on doctor's orders' the passengers had applied for and consumed 11 gallons of spirits, 21 gallons of wine and 1,190 bottles of ale/stout which comprised the entire stock of 'medicinal liquor' on board. One wonders if these 'medicinal activities' extended to a dance and some cigars too.

In 1924, it was decided that *Caronia* and her sister ship *Carmania* would be converted to burn oil instead of coal as the new route to Canada was established, with other ships in the Cunard fleet following. This would involve the two liners heading into Barrow to have this conversion carried out.

However, it seems that drama was never far away. In February 1927, once again *Caronia* was involved in an incident at sea as she came across a burning sailing vessel, a schooner that had apparently been abandoned. It was thought that it might have been a rum runner, the crew having escaped in a motorboat and leaving it to sink, after no sign of human life was found. *Caronia* carried on her journey as normal. This turned out to be a voyage full of incident because since she had left Liverpool on 5 February she had suffered a fire in a Third Class cabin, a hatch had been damaged in a storm, a woman had given birth to a stillborn baby, assistance had been given to a ship that had an injured crew member on board in heavy seas and she had to slow down significantly in a blizzard heading out of New York for Boston. It was at this point, when she was heading out of Boston, that the schooner was sighted before the ship continued eastbound for Queenstown and Liverpool.

In 1928, *Caronia* was used as a hotel and accommodated around 300 guests for the annual Grand National horse race, expecting to host them on board for two days. Special events were being held on board to entertain guests during their stay and to make sure they stayed for as long as possible, the scheduled sailing on the Saturday being delayed by four hours as a consequence. By this time the ship had been placed on a route taking her to Havana, Cuba, a voyage that filled the cabins without issue on her first journey there despite other lines having to make significant efforts to attract passengers. However, the United States Shipping Board was soon warned of Cunard's intention to take legal action when they placed the rival liner *President Roosevelt* on the Havana route, which Cunard said violated the Federal Shipping Act of 1920. By January the following year there was a report (that was later denied) that there was a wager on who would reach Havana first, with the prize being $1,000 for the first ship to dock there.

On 8 February 1929, tragedy once again hit *Caronia* as the ship entered New York minus her surgeon. Dr Harold Trenchard Rossiter, aged forty-six and from Stubbington in Hampshire, vanished overboard just before the ship entered port. He left behind his wife Madeline who he had been married to for just under nine years.

Two years later, Southampton resident Stuart Fisher, aged forty-four, went overboard as the ship came into New York on 29 August 1931. His body was not found for over a week, eventually being retrieved from the Hudson River.

Once again, the effect of the Great Depression on worldwide shipping sealed the fate of *Caronia*. It was decided that she should be sold off for scrapping along with her sister ship *Carmania*. Purchased by Hughes Bolckows in Blythe, she arrived there on 20 May 1932 and was soon sold on once more to a Japanese company and was waiting to be taken away when some further concerns emerged. In December 1932, she was alongside the port when it was found that working machinery had suffered considerable damage to dynamos after sulphuric acid had been found to have corroded major parts. Police were called when suspicions were raised that this could be a case of sabotage, the destruction of the *Empress of Scotland* two years previously still fresh in the minds of those raising suspicion of foul play.

For her last voyage she was renamed and became *Taiseiyo Maru* before being taken to Osaka in Japan where she was broken up the following year.

20

Noordam

Type	Liner
Length	550.3 feet
Gross tonnage	12,316
Built	Harland & Wolff, Belfast
Owners	Holland-America Line
Link to *Titanic*	Ice warnings relayed to ships in area

Launched on 28 September 1901, the twin screw steamship *Noordam* was completed by the end of March 1902 and soon set sail on her maiden voyage on 1 May on her regular route between Rotterdam and New York. Inside she had all the luxuries of the larger liners: a First Class area, library, smoking room and elegant dining rooms, the cabins giving her passengers a taste of Dutch hospitality while journeying across the cold grey Atlantic at around 15 knots.

She was painted with the standard black hull, her single funnel in company colours of dark yellow with blue and white stripes gave this vessel her identity from a distance. On board she could carry up to 286 in First Class, 292 in Second Class and 1,800 in Third Class.

Under the command of Captain Watze Krol, *Noordam* was making her usual transatlantic voyage on 14 April 1912 when she started to encounter a significant amount of ice in the area. Krol, the thirty-nine-year-old Dutch veteran of the line, had spent over twenty years with Holland-America since he was a cadet and he had been in command of this ship since October 1911. There was no real concern, the ship and captain had been through this before, so it was just a simple case of keeping a sharp lookout and making sure the bergs were noted down and warnings sent to other ships.

At 1140 hours on that Sunday morning, *Noordam* transmitted her ice warning that was relayed by the *Caronia* to *Titanic*, telling them of ice at 42N 49 to 51W, before continuing on her journey. When *Titanic* struck ice just twelve hours later *Noordam* was many miles away from the disaster and did not go to the scene. The ice report itself had only a passing mention at the later inquiries.

Noordam's service during the First World War was interesting. A month after war was declared she was captured Mid-Atlantic and escorted into Queenstown by a British cruiser and 125 German prisoners were then taken off. However, this was not the only drama for her during the war, as she would be damaged twice in three years. The first time was on 17 October 1914 when she was travelling in the North Sea and suddenly the ship was struck by a huge explosion as a mine detonated. There were no fatalities but several on board

A postcard featuring *Noordam*. (Author)

were injured. The repairs at Rotterdam took until early the following year to complete and she only resumed sailing again on 26 March 1915.

As the war dragged on in 1916, mail on *Noordam* and *Vandyk* was detained by the authorities in New York, leaving the ships' mail services significantly delayed. This was not the first time this had happened. In December 1915, *Noordam*'s mail and that of two other ships had been seized in Britain, much to the outrage of the Dutch government.

The second incident in which *Noordam* was damaged by a mine occurred on 3 August 1917. On this time occasion she was a bit closer to home, only 14 miles from the Dutch coast, in what was thought to be a safe area for ships to transit. The 250 passengers evacuated the ship in lifeboats and were safely away from the ship. A nearby torpedo boat left the port of Terschelling to render assistance while relatives of those on board eagerly waited in the harbour at Helder, the swiftness of the evacuation seeing one woman, a Mrs Pleyte, come ashore in pyjamas. *Noordam* went back to Rotterdam for more patching up, which was not completed until March 1919, by which time the war was over and she had been put on the Rotterdam to New York route via Plymouth and Brest.

The Swedish-American Line took over the running of *Noordam* in March 1923 and she was renamed *Kungsholm* and placed on the Gothenburg to New York route. Her passenger cabin capacity also changed, and now she had room for 563 in Cabin Class and a further 1,468 in Third Class accommodation. Three years later she was taken back to her original owners who promptly reinstated her old name back and once again *Noordam* was back at sea carrying just Third Class passengers. A small announcement in the newspapers in

Another postcard featuring *Noordam*. (Author)

August 1922 announced that *Noordam* had encountered a spate of bad weather which had not only delayed her by twenty-four hours, but had also seen her struck by lightning on the foremast – a scary situation if you are on watch in a crow's nest.

By April 1927 she was quite an old ship and was finally withdrawn from service. The breaking up of the vessel for scrap commenced at Waalhaven in 1928 before she was towed over to Hendrik Ido Ambacht for the rest of her hull to be dismantled. So ended the long and colourful life of SS *Noordam*.

21

Samson

Type	Seal hunting vessel
Length	147 feet, 9 inches
Gross tonnage	506
Built	K. Larsen, Logebergskaret, Norway
Owners	A/S Saelfangerdampskibet Samson
Link to *Titanic*	Theory of *Samson* being the mystery ship between *Titanic* and *Californian*

Launched in 1885, the Norwegian sealing vessel *Samson* was officially classed as a barque, although she was also a steamship, with one funnel almost hidden behind the three tall masts that towered over her white hull. A fairly small vessel, *Samson* was built for the cold weather and could power along at around 7 knots, not a great speed but if you were on board the *Samson* you were not there for a quick journey anywhere.

Samson went through a number of owners in a very short period of time, each one under the partnership of Handelshuset Thommesen. She would head out to the freezing Arctic areas carrying a total of forty-five crew along with eight small boats to hunt seals. In 1908, she was sold to Auguste Fosse and her port of registry changed from Arendal to Trondheim. In 1912, the *Samson* was not even mentioned in *Titanic* circles and never came up at any inquiry or featured in any press reports.

It wasn't until fifty years after the sinking of *Titanic* that *Samson*'s involvement in the disaster came to light when a deathbed confession by First Officer Henrik Bergethon Naess was revealed in a BBC documentary. He claimed that on the night of the sinking *Samson* had been engaged in activities involving the transportation of 3,000 lb of seal meat that had been illegally hunted in Canadian waters. Observing the distressed *Titanic* and having no wireless radio, *Samson* turned away and ignored the cries for help when the rockets went up. Instead of rendering assistance, the ship quietly slipped away, hoping to remain undetected by the authorities.

Although Naess was generally regarded as a credible person, his story had many holes in it. These were soon picked apart, namely why were they in that area if they were hunting off Canada? In addition, Naess had already confessed to this before on several occasions and had repeatedly changed his story, and none of the other crew members had ever mentioned it. While it is highly unlikely that *Samson* was in the vicinity of the sinking *Titanic*, his account offered a small crumb of hope for those wanting to clear the name of Captain Lord of *Californian*. However, there is no evidence to prove if *Samson* was in the area or not, and therefore Naess's story must be taken with a pinch of salt.

Samson carried on operating as a sealer and in 1914 was sold to the Canadian Whaling Co. Ltd and renamed *Jacobsen*. Five years later, the ship was sold again to Swedish owners and renamed *Bellsund* before a further name change in 1928 when she assumed her old name of *Samson* once more. When the Swedish owners sold her to American explorer Richard E. Byrd a year later, *Samson* was once again renamed as *City of New York*. She also took on a new role as a cold weather exploration ship for Byrd's icebound expeditions.

Byrd's Antarctic expeditions hit the headlines around the world, making *Samson* famous. After a number of successful voyages, the vessel was moored in New York and became a museum about the expeditions. In 1932, *City of New York* was on display at the Chicago World's Fair and the year after that President Franklin Roosevelt came aboard while he was in the Great Lakes area.

In the Second World War, the former sealer was converted to a schooner and operated up and down the Canadian coast. By the end of the war, this work had taken its toll, and she was showing her age having experienced several technical problems. *City of New York* was eventually sold to be used for general transportation of potatoes and coal but ran aground on 29 December 1952 off Nova Scotia. A cabin stove went over in the chaos and a fire broke out, the ship burning for several days before sinking where she had grounded. It was another ten years before *Samson* was made famous once again by being linked to the *Titanic* and *Californian* incident.

Above left and left: Samson. (Author unknown)

Above right: Samson in drydock at Georgernes Verft. (Author unknown)

22

Amerika

Type	Liner
Length	669 feet
Gross tonnage	22,622
Built	Harland & Wolff, Belfast
Owners	Hamburg-America Line, Hamburg
Link to *Titanic* story	Transmitted ice warnings in area

Launched on 20 April 1905, *Amerika* was officially the heaviest ship in the world at the time and several thousand people turned up to see her slide into the waters at the Belfast shipyard. She was soon towed over to be fitted out and upon completion made her maiden voyage on 11 October that year on the Hamburg to New York route via Dover. This trip attracted a lot of attention from senior figures in the shipping and building company as well as dignitaries from the Dover area and even a German Prince, all of whom came on board for a tour of this magnificent new floating palace. Looking much like many of the other Belfast-built liners of her era from the outside, she had four masts broken up by two funnels in the middle, her company colours of dark orange giving away the ship's identity from afar. She could carry over 2,500 passengers in four classes with a crew of 577 to cater for them, ships of this type being more like emigrant ships than luxury liners. By 3 November that year *Amerika* had returned to Britain. Despite her arrival being delayed for two days due to bad gales out at sea, she sailed into Plymouth to the delight of the crowds of people who had turned up just to look at this huge liner.

Amerika had quite a fan following from the start as there were few ships that were as big as her. This was particularly so in Germany and visits to the ship by members of the public increased. In 1906, the kaiser himself made a trip to Cuxhaven to view her along with his usual entourage. The popularity of the ship meant that her newly launched sister ship *Kaiserin Auguste Victoria* would do just as well.

In July 1910, the liner come under scrutiny following two thefts on board, both cases in which jewels were stolen from passengers. In the first incident, $5,000 worth of jewels were taken from two passengers who reported it straight away, but after a search of the ship no trace of them or the culprit was found. Three weeks later, £10,000 of jewels was stolen from the cabin of an American woman, and this was reported to the police in Hamburg as the ship came into port. Robberies by organised criminal gangs on these larger ships during transatlantic voyages were becoming almost commonplace, but those responsible were seemingly not being apprehended for their crimes.

In April 1912, *Amerika* was on a voyage from New York to her home port of Hamburg in Germany under the command of Captain Knuth when the crew of *Amerika* reported the sighting of ice in the Mid-Atlantic. Like many other ships in the area, her radio room transmitted a number of warnings to nearby vessels. On 14 April at 1120 hours, the US Hydrographic Office (callsign MXG) received a transmission from *Amerika* warning of ice in the vicinity of 41.27N 50.08W. *Titanic* picked up this message, one of many that were being transmitted that create a picture of the icy hazards right in *Titanic's* path. It is possible that this message was not relayed to the bridge as the radio operators were dealing with a vast amount of personal traffic, according to investigators. The loss of *Titanic* stunned the ocean liner industry and the role of *Amerika* in the ice warnings was duly noted, yet they could have done no more than they did.

This was not the first maritime disaster that *Amerika* would be linked to that year. In the early hours of 4 October 1912, the Royal Navy submarine *B-2* was taking part in exercises with other units, including submarine *C-17*, and was running on the surface when *Amerika* approached on her way to Dover after crossing over from New York. The submarine was showing running lights and although on the surface and in clear weather, the bow of the liner sliced into her forward hull section and she sank with the loss of fifteen crew. There was only one survivor, an officer, who was thrown clear of the sinking boat because he was on the bridge at the time of the collision. *Amerika* stopped nearby and lowered lifeboats in an attempt to search for survivors but there was no escape for the crew of the submarine who

Left: Amerika. (Bain Photo Service)

Opposite above: A postcard featuring *Amerika*. (Author)

Opposite below: The Royal Navy submarine *B-2* sunk in collision with the *Amerika*. (From *Popular Mechanics* magazine, 1913)

were trapped inside. *Amerika* continued to Southampton, anchoring outside of Southampton Water that morning where Captain Knuth and the crew gave statements to an inquiry team. An investigation laid full blame with the crew of *Amerika*, singling out the Second Officer in particular for not seeing the submarine, not take greater precautions and for posting inadequate lookouts. The owners paid damages for the lost submarine, which was settled, but this did not bring the lost submariners back. As for the wreck of *B-2*, she was discovered by divers many years later and positively identified in an expedition in 1999.

Upon the outbreak of the First World War, *Amerika* found herself alongside in Boston, Massachusetts, which was a neutral port at the time. It was decided to stay there to avoid being seized by the British. However, when the US entered the war in 1917 the liner was promptly seized and renamed USS *America* to be used as a troop transport ship. On one trip in winter 1918 during the Spanish flu pandemic, the ship had over 1,000 cases of flu on board, affecting both the crew and soldiers in transit. While the ship was isolated at anchor

off the French port of Brest, the doctors on board worked hard to prevent the spread of the disease. However, fifty-five embarked personnel died and many others were left too weak to do anything until their bodies eventually fought off the virus.

There were more challenges ahead for *America* in 1918. On 15 October, she was alongside her pier at Hoboken, New Jersey, being filled with coal when in the early hours of the morning she started to list. Water poured in through the coal ports and the alarm was raised to evacuate the liner. She slowly sank in an upright position as her hull settled on the bed of the harbour, a salvage operation now necessary to try and refloat her. Thankfully, everybody managed to get off the ship before she went down.

It took just over a month for salvage crews to pump the water out and have her refloated again, on 21 November 1918, just ten days after the end of the war. The repairs to the liner were carried out and she was back in service just a few months later. Although the war was over, the use of her as a troopship went on long after hostilities had ceased. The ship was eventually returned to normal service in 1920. A year later *America* was under the ownership of the United States Line where *America* and plying the New York to Bremen via Plymouth and Cherbourg route.

After several years of steady operation, *America* was alongside Newport News, Virginia, on 10 March 1926 when a fire broke out during the final phase of her reconditioning. The fire spread quickly and burned for seven hours, putting the date she would be returned to her owners back even further while the repairs to this new damage were carried out.

When *America* eventually got back to sea she was under the command of Captain George Fried and heading to New York on 22 January 1929 in a ferocious storm. Suddenly, the ship was in receipt of distress calls that had been transmitted from the steamer *Florida* somewhere off the eastern coast of the US. Using her radio direction finder, *America* searched the seas for the stricken ship and after many hours came across *Florida* and proceeded to rescue the thirty-two people on board using their lifeboat and sending over

SS *America*. (William J. Craig)

USS *Amerika* sunk. (National Archives USA)

nine crew led by Chief Officer Harry Manning. When news reached the shore, *America*'s crew were honoured for their bravery with a celebratory parade. Manning later became captain of another liner named *America*. He also flew with Amelia Earhart on several occasions and would have been lost if he hadn't left her crew just before her final flight and disappearance in 1937.

By the time the Second World War was in full swing in Europe, *America* had been laid up in Maryland on the Patuxent River in a reserve fleet for a while. By the end of 1940, she would be used as a floating barracks and renamed *Edmund B. Alexander* so that she would not be confused with another liner of the same name currently under construction. The following year she lost one of her funnels in an overhaul and bore little resemblance to the ship that had been out on the night of the *Titanic* disaster.

Making several journeys across the Atlantic carrying US troops to the Mediterranean and being a part of the convoy system, she was a prized possession that needed protection at all costs. An attack on *Edmund B. Alexander* would have been disastrous. Even after the war she became a victim of the conflict when striking a mine off Bremerhaven in 1946. The damaged vessel was towed into port and the repairs were quickly carried out.

The story of the former *Amerika* came to an end with her being placed in reserve once again in 1949 on the Hudson River. She would call this place home until she was sold for breaking up on 16 January 1957 and towed to Baltimore to be scrapped soon after. So ended a ship that had served in two world wars, fighting against the country that she had originally been destined to serve.

23

Prinz Adalbert

Type	Liner
Length	403.3 feet
Gross tonnage	6,030
Built	Bremer Vulkan Schiffbau & Machinen Fabrik, Germany
Owners	Hamburg-America Line
Link to *Titanic* story	Photographs taken onboard possibly show the icebergs that sank *Titanic*

Launched on 21 August 1902, the German liner *Prinz Adalbert* was built for the transatlantic passenger trade. She could accommodate a grand total of 1,260 people in First Class and Third Class. After her fitting out was completed, her maiden voyage from her home port of Hamburg to Brazil commenced on 20 January the following year.

Taking on several routes between Europe and the Americas, she was on a routine crossing on the morning of 16 April 1912 after *Titanic* had gone down when she encountered ice in the area. As news of the disaster had not reached the ship, the crew were therefore unaware of what had happened in this area and the significance of the ice that around the ship.

As the ship came close by, Chief Steward Linoenewald took out a camera and photographed one particular iceberg, a huge beast with three prongs almost resembling Neptune's trident. *Prinz Adalbert* passed by slowly while those on the upper deck marvelled at this freezing wonder of nature. As the ship came close, the crew noticed red marks that looked like paint scrapings down one side of the berg, almost as if a vessel had collided with it leaving behind marks of the hull. When news of what had happened to *Titanic* reached the ship, it became obvious just what they had seen. That photograph became the most famous iceberg photo in history and has been recreated in all *Titanic* films as the likely candidate that sank the grandest ship in the world.

Later, four crewmen, including Linoenewald, signed a statement that included the following passage:

> On the day after the sinking of the *Titanic*, the steamer *Prinz Adalbert* passes the iceberg shown in this photograph. The *Titanic* disaster was not yet known by us. On one side red paint was plainly visible, which has the appearance of having been made by the scraping of a vessel on the iceberg. SS *Prinz Adalbert* Hamburg America Line.

It is interesting that a ship only two days' travel away from the site of the disaster did not hear of the sinking. This was almost the only news going over the airwaves at the time, with radio stations across the Atlantic picking up messages and information about the sinking. How did *Prinz Adalbert* in the Mid-Atlantic not hear anything about this?

At the outbreak of the First World War the liner was seized in Falmouth by Britain, one of over a hundred German vessels taken as a war prize. She was renamed *Princetown* two years later. By 1917, she had new owners across the Channel, Cie Sud Atlantique, and was once again renamed, this time *Alesia*. She was managed by Gellatly, Hankey & Co., but she was not with her new owners for long. On 5 September 1917, the German submarine *UC-69* sighted *Alesia* while she was on a voyage from Cardiff to Bordeaux, carrying general cargo and coal. The U-boat torpedoed the ship 40 miles north-west of Ushant but only damaged her before withdrawing. The following day another submarine found her and torpedoes from *UC-50* sent the ship to the bottom.

In October 2015, the famous photo of the iceberg was put up for auction by Henry Aldridge & Son in Wiltshire, along with many other items of *Titanic* memorabilia. The bidding was tough, but the image was eventually sold for an incredible £21,000, a much higher figure than expected. Who would have thought a simple iceberg photograph without any knowledge of its significance would have caused so many outward ripples over a century on?

Prinz Adalbert. (Ships Nostalgia)

The famous iceberg photograph taken aboard *Prinz Adalbert*. (Wikimedia commons)

24

Niagara

Type	Ocean liner
Length	485 feet
Gross tonnage	8,481
Built	Ateliers & Chantiers de La Noire, St Nazaire, France
Owners	Compagnie Generale Transatlantique
Link to *Titanic* story	Collided with iceberg days before *Titanic*

There have been several ships named *Niagara*, the most famous one being sunk full of gold and becoming the focus of a well-told story of treasure and salvage. However, her predecessor had a much quieter life in comparison. Launched on 16 May 1908 originally as the *Corse* for the French company Chargeurs Reunis, she made her maiden voyage the following year. She was sold not long after to Compagnie Generale Transatlantique, better known as the French Line, in 1910 and renamed *Niagara*.

Niagara could carry 1,142 passengers (182 in First Class and 960 in Third Class) and her steam triple-expansion engines were able to push the single-funnelled liner at a reasonable speed of 15 knots on the Bordeaux and Le Havre to New York service. By 1912, this French liner was no stranger to crossing the Atlantic and became something of a sideline in *Titanic*'s story because of an event that occurred in almost the same area and had implications for the disaster that was to unfold.

On 10 April 1912, *Niagara* was halfway through her voyage westbound under the command of Captain Juhan. She was six days into her final voyage on the Le Havre to New York route at exactly the same time *Titanic*, thousands of miles away, sailed on her maiden voyage from Southampton. *Niagara* had come upon ice in the reported position of 44.39N 48.30W and despite all best efforts the ship collided with it. This caused damage to the ship, her bow now buckled and holed. After a brief check to make sure the ship was safe to carry on, reports came back that although there was slight damage, it would be wise to proceed when ready.

Continuing with the voyage, *Niagara* arrived in New York several days later and had her repairs carried out. She would sail again as planned to commence her new route, Le Havre across the Atlantic to Quebec and Montreal.

Looking at the *Niagara* incident, the reports of icebergs that were later described as 'in the vicinity' of where *Titanic* went down should be taken with a pinch of salt because of discrepancies in the time it took for the ships to get to and from the area in question and how fast they were travelling. Examining the evidence, the damage could not have been

A postcard featuring *Niagara*. (Author)

that bad as the ship was back at sea soon after and therefore it is most likely that the iceberg *Niagara* hit was many miles away from where *Titanic* would eventually sink. This incident would probably not even have been mentioned in the papers if the events of four days later had not taken place.

Niagara had a busy yet unremarkable career at sea after this, her route being changed several times over the years and taking her to Hamburg, Bordeaux, New York and Havana among many other destinations. Her final voyage was on 17 March 1930 from Le Havre to New York and she was scrapped in 1931.

25

Frankfurt

Type	Liner
Length	430.3 feet
Gross tonnage	7,341
Built	J. C. Tecklenborg Actien Gesselschaft, Germany
Owners	Norddeutscher Lloyd Line
Link to *Titanic* story	Picked up *Titanic* distress call and came to assist

Frankfurt was another German liner to feature in the story of *Titanic*. Built in 1899 and launched on 17 December of that year, her maiden voyage was from Bremen to Baltimore on 31 March 1900, just three months after being put in the water. With her single funnel coloured buff in the Norddeutscher company colours, she could cross the Atlantic at a reasonable speed of 12.5 knots with almost 2,000 passengers on board when fully loaded.

By 1912, she was making regular trips between Bremen and the US. On 15 April, she was heading east to Bremerhaven after a port visit to Galveston, Texas, and very early that morning she picked up the distress call from *Titanic* giving her position as 41.44N 50.24W. *Frankfurt* wireless operator W. Zippel replied with simply 'standby'. The ship was thought to be around 150 miles from that location and would not be able to offer any assistance, although there has been speculation that she was in fact closer due to the signal strength of the messages being picked up. This has been much debated by historians but is impossible to verify. *Titanic* replied to *Frankfurt* with 'you are a fool, keep yourself away!' when the German ship kept asking questions, but the ability to transmit messages was soon lost as the ship began to sink.

However, *Frankfurt* was still the first ship to acknowledge the message of distress from *Titanic* and until another one did, she was turned around and headed to the scene of the emergency. Captain Hattorff ordered full speed and preparations to receive any survivors that might be found in the water. Blankets were assembled and the galley opened up to make bread. In the freezing temperatures it was anybody's guess how many survivors there might be.

However, *Frankfurt* would be many hours too late, *Carpathia* having rescued everybody by late morning when the German liner eventually arrived on the scene. However, *Frankfurt* did inform *Californian* of the disaster via her radio. Inaccurate reports in the coming days stated that *Frankfurt* was actually 20 miles closer to *Titanic* than *Carpathia*, but this was incorrect. However, a number of people came forward to substantiate this, including the evidence submitted by *Titanic*'s radio operator Harold Bride. Captain Hattorff stated that

SS *Frankfurt*. (Unknown)

Frankfurt arrived on the scene at 1050 that morning and observed *Carpathia*, *Birma* and *Virginian* already there as well as seventeen small icebergs among huge icefields. However, contrary to this evidence, the captain of *Virginian* stated that *Frankfurt* was not sighted at all. Captain Hattorff kept his ship on the scene until noon before continuing with the voyage, which looking at the timings means that *Frankfurt* was only there for just over an hour. He blamed the amount of ice for making a further search 'useless', according to newspaper reports.

Four months after the *Titanic* disaster, *Frankfurt* found herself in a drama of her own. On 11 August 1912, she was on a voyage from Bremen to Canada with 1,200 emigrants on board when she was in a collision with another German steamer, *Barmen*, off the Hook of Holland, 20 miles from land. The damage sustained caused flooding below decks, although the ship was not in any danger of sinking, and 740 passengers had to be taken off and transferred to the nearby steamship *Juno*. *Frankfurt* had to be towed by four tugs into Maasluis, near Rotterdam, for repairs. Thankfully, none of the passengers and crew on board were in any danger. In the meantime, *Barmen* had limped into Rotterdam with her bows crumpled inwards. Both ships were later repaired and soon back in service.

Like many German ships, *Frankfurt* was surrendered to Britain at the end of First World War and taken over by the White Star Line in 1919. She was sold on to the Oriental Navigation Company in Hong Kong three years later and renamed *Sarvistan*. Less than a decade later, the former *Frankfurt* was taken to Japan for scrapping, arriving there in 1931. Frankfurt Seamount, one of the Grand Banks seamounts, was named after this *Titanic* rescue ship despite her not having been able to assist and arriving too late to partake in the rescue.

26

Virginian

Type	Liner
Length	538 feet
Gross tonnage	10,754
Built	Alexander Stephen and Sons, Glasgow
Owners	Allan Line
Link to *Titanic* Story	Responded to distress calls

Launched as the SS *Virginian* on 22 December 1904, she made her maiden voyage on 6 April 1905 from Liverpool for the transatlantic voyage to Canada. Her black hull sported a single funnel with the company colours of red with a white stripe and a standard black tip. She had the ability to carry 426 First Class, 286 Second Class and around 1,000 Third Class passengers as her triple screws pushed her along at a top speed of 18 knots.

Virginian's early voyages were a huge success, and the ship made headlines when she steamed across the Atlantic twenty-four hours faster than her sister ship *Victorian*. She would continue on to other ports in record times, averaging the expected 18 knots along the way. On one occasion, her new turbine engines pushed her across the Atlantic in an astonishing six days, twenty-two hours and twenty minutes and that despite heavy seas. A later voyage saw her speeding along at 19½ to 20 knots for over 2,000 miles.

By September 1905 reports stated that *Virginian* was ashore on Crane Island in Canada and in a 'leaky condition'. However, this was an erroneous report and referred to a Leyland liner of the same name. Ironically, *Virginian*'s Allan Line sister ship *Victorian* went aground two days later not far away this area, so perhaps the confusion in the press could be forgiven.

Virginian was not only a reliable ship but was frequented by important people. The Canadian prime minister, for example, used her to travel to Britain for a conference in 1911, a momentous occasion that was celebrated by crowds of people milling around the ship with bunting fluttering in the breeze.

On 15 April 1912, *Virginian* was 178 miles away from the sinking *Titanic* and heading eastbound when she heard Cape Race relay the distress call. Captain Gambell turned the ship towards the position indicated and sped to the scene of the disaster. *Titanic*'s distress signals soon began to reach *Virginian* as she got closer but at 0157 hours the signals suddenly stopped. By then *Titanic*'s power had failed and she was making the final plunge to the seabed not long after.

Although the ship was too far away to render any assistance in the end, the false reports getting to the press on shore told stories of survivors being loaded aboard *Virginian*. It was even reported that *Titanic* was being towed to safety by *Virginian* and everybody had got off the ship alive.

When the liner reached the reported position there was nothing to be seen that gave any hint that the *Titanic* had ever been there – no wreckage, no bodies, no survivors. With no assistance to render, the *Virginian* turned back to resume her original course and continued on her voyage. With the ambiguity over the role of *Virginian* being transmitted over the airways, it gave false hope to those wondering what the fate of *Titanic* was as well as confusion when it came to the chain of events that were taking place mid-ocean. Nobody really knows the origins of the false stories but they resulted in some newspapers putting the report of *Virginian* towing *Titanic* to safety on their front pages. The American newspaper the *Evening Sun* announced 'All Titanic Passengers Are Safe'. Further details in the reports described how all the passengers were being transferred to *Virginian* and *Carpathia*, while a line was being passed to the crippled *Titanic*. Needless to say, when the truth was revealed, it came as a huge shock.

In 1914, *Virginian* became loosely involved with another major disaster, the sinking of the liner *Empress of Ireland* following a collision. The Allan Line ship was chartered by Canadian Pacific to continue on that route as the replacement ship. Months later that charter ended as the First World War broke out and *Virginian* was fitted out as a troop transport and rigged as an Armed Merchant Cruiser, now known as HMS *Virginian*.

Throughout the war *Virginian* took part in various patrols and convoy duties. On 19 August 1917, the submarine *U-102* fired a torpedo into her side, killing three crew. Thankfully, she stayed afloat and limped into port for repairs. During the war, she lost ten personnel and on cessation of hostilities *Virginian* was once again handed over to Canadian Pacific (which had been taken over by the Allan Line) and resumed her regular passenger service.

The Swedish America Line purchased the ship in 1920 and renamed her *Drottningholm*, amending her steerage passengers to just 700, Second Class to 300 and First Class replaced with 280 Cabin Class. This led to many Swedish migrants making the journey to the US on board her and the Atlantic trips continued as before. As the years went by, she was painted white, including her funnel, and looked very different to her original set-up. Some prominent passengers included the 1932 Los Angeles Summer Olympics team from Sweden and actress Greta Garbo to name but a few.

In 1923, members of the Swedish parliament, the Riksdag, made a tour of the harbour and had tea on board the liner, much to their delight. On 28 February 1939, the ship

A postcard featuring *Virginian*. (Author)

performed a rescue operation when the sealing vessel *Isfjell* was in distress off Greenland in bad weather. *Drottningholm*'s lifeboat was launched, enabling the Swedes to save the sealer's crew of twenty as the 94-foot-long ship went down.

Sweden was neutral during the Second World War and passenger services to the US continued. In 1942, it was revealed that German-born American citizen Herbert Karl Friedrich, who had arrived on board, was arrested as a spy when he reached the US, much to the delight of the press reporting it. By the following year, the ship was being used to ferry British and German prisoners back to their homelands after agreements were reached to send home the wounded via Sweden as a midway point. *Drottningholm* took prisoners through the Baltic and into the North Sea to Britain. Thousands of prisoners had spent several years in camps across enemy territory and were now overjoyed to be back on British soil, the same being said of the Germans going in the opposite direction.

On 28 February 1946, *Drottningholm* was in Liverpool dockyard after arriving from Sweden and was due to sail to India the day after when fire broke out on board in the early hours of the morning. Fifty fire units were called out to deal with the blaze as passengers and crew evacuated the ship onto the dockside buildings, where they spent the rest of the night. One woman suffered the effects of smoke inhalation and had to be revived but other than that there were no real casualties among the passengers and crew. It appeared that the fire had started in a cargo hold aft, spreading onto nearby cotton bales in No. 5 hold. Five members of the fire teams were overcome by fumes and smoke. This was one of three ship fires that night in the same dockyard.

By 1948 the *Drottningholm* had been sold and renamed *Brasil* by South American owners, although there is confusion as to the name of the company that took over. Three years later, Hamburg-America Line chartered her and renamed her *Homeland* for a new route from Germany to the US via Southampton and Halifax, with trips to the Mediterranean thrown in. Her passenger capacity was again reduced considerably to 96 First Class and 846 Tourist Class. Times had changed and so had the roles of ocean liners like this ship.

By the time her life came to an end in 1955, she was almost the last surviving ship to have a link to *Titanic* (the other being the tender *Nomadic*). The former *Virginian* was taken away and scrapped at Trieste in Italy later that year.

Another postcard featuring *Virginian*. (Author)

27

Birma

Type	Liner
Length	415 feet
Gross tonnage	4,661
Built	Fairfield & Co. Ltd, Glasgow
Owners	Russian American Line
Link to *Titanic* story	Responded to distress call

Launched as *Arundel Castle* on 2 October 1894 for the Union-Castle Line, this liner made her maiden voyage from London to Natal in south-east Africa the following year. She operated as a general long-distance liner until she was sold to the East Asiatic Company in 1905 and renamed *Birma*. Three years later, she was under the ownership of the Russian American Line and running between the Netherlands and the USA, carrying 200 First Class, 100 Second Class and up to 1,150 Third Class passengers.

Not a particularly memorable vessel, *Birma* looked like any other liner of the period, a single funnel with four masts being a common sight in the ports on either side of the Atlantic. On one of her journeys eastbound to Libau via Rotterdam the ship became

HS *Mitava*, formerly *Birma*. (Unknown)

involved in the most famous shipwreck in history. At 0030 hours on 15 April 1912, *Birma* was around 100 miles away from the sinking *Titanic* when the distress call was picked up:

> CQD – SOS From MGY
> We have stuck iceberg sinking fast come to our assistance.
> Position Lat. 41.46N Lon. 50.14W

For seventy-three years this position was accepted as the final location of *Titanic*. The time and date given in the message, 1145 on 14 April, is different to that stated by *Birma* because the ships were in different time zones. The radio operator of *Birma* rushed the signal to the bridge despite not knowing at the time the name of the ship in question. *Titanic*'s callsign of MGY was not in their identification books yet as it was so new, and the nearby *Frankfurt* had to confirm with them that this message was from the new White Star liner *Titanic*.

The message was immediately taken seriously and *Birma* was turned onto a new course and headed at full speed towards the position indicated in the signal. Another message was received by *Birma* at around 0140 hours:

> SOS SOS CQD CQD – MGY
> We are sinking fast passengers being put into boats
> MGY

A frustrating night ended at 0730 hours later that morning when the ship arrived near the co-ordinates, ice preventing her from getting any closer and *Carpathia* already nearby. On offering assistance to the Cunarder, the response was 'shut up'. *Birma*'s wireless operator, Joseph Cannon, probably realised that it was Marconi Company policy not to provide information to ships that had a rival wireless system. *Birma* was fitted with a De Forest Wireless Telegraph system while most other ships had the Marconi radio. In any event, *Carpathia* was coming to the end of her rescue operation.

With no work left to do, *Birma* turned back onto her original course and continued her journey. A member of the crew took a photograph of an iceberg that looked very much like the one that has gone down in history as 'the iceberg' responsible for the sinking. In the meantime, somehow rumours persisted that *Birma* had on board five lifeboats from *Titanic*. The ship was forced to issue a denial and that all hope was resting on other ships finding survivors. Sadly, this was not to be.

The ice warnings were brought up at the inquiry and the position given was the one that went down in history as the exact location until it was contradicted by Ballard's discovery of the wreck of *Titanic* in 1985.

In 1913, *Birma* was renamed *Mitau* and was laid up at Kronstadt in Russia at the outbreak of the First World War a year later. By 1919 she had reverted to the name *Birma* under the East Asiatic Steamship Company and was sold two years after that to the Polish Navigation Company and renamed *Josef Pilsudski*, after the prominent Polish general. By the end of 1921 she was being held in Kiel over the failure to pay a number of repair bills. After the company who owned her was liquidated, in 1922 the new German owners renamed her yet again, this time *Wilbo*. Eventually, she was taken to Genoa in Italy where she was scrapped in 1924.

28

Parisian

Type	Liner
Length	440.8 feet
Gross tonnage	5,395
Built	Napier and Sons, Glasgow
Owners	Allan Line
Link to *Titanic* story	A ship in vicinity that received radio traffic from *Titanic*

SS *Parisian* was a minor player in the *Titanic* story but helps build up a picture of just how many vessels were in that area on the night of the disaster.

Launched from her slipway in Glasgow on 4 November 1880, the single-funnelled liner (although, originally, she had two) started out her maiden voyage on 10 March 1881 from Liverpool to Boston via Halifax. She had a number of transatlantic voyages under her belt long before her Marconi radio was installed in 1902.

At dusk on 25 March 1905, *Parisian* was heading into Halifax harbour and taking on board the pilot when another liner was sighted also heading inbound. The Hamburg-America liner *Albano* was not slowing down or giving way and as *Parisian* slowly started to make her way into the harbour, *Albano* sliced into the starboard side of her. Between the two

Parisian. (Author)

Parisian at Quebec. (Author)

ships they had nearly 2,200 people on board and now both had sustained damage to their hulls, *Parisian*'s significantly worse than that of *Albano*. The *Parisian* crew worked hard to pump out the influx of water down below and placed collision mats over the holes in the hull, saving the ship. Incredibly, there were no injuries. By now every ship in the nearby harbour was on standby to give assistance but thankfully it was not required. The two ships were brought alongside where repairs could be carried out once an investigation was completed. A later inquiry by a Canadian court apportioned the blame solely with *Albano*.

Seven years later and *Parisian* set sail from Glasgow on 6 April 1912 bound for Boston via Halifax under the command of Captain Hains. On the night of 14 April, she transmitted a general position message saying simply '50 miles west-southwest' of *Titanic*, which the White Star liner acknowledged, the ship steadily making her way west at her best speed. Radio operator Sutherland shut his radio down that night and did not turn it back on until 0800 hours the following morning and by then *Titanic* had gone and he heard nothing but traffic regarding this disaster on the airwaves. At the time of the disaster *Parisian* was estimated to be around 150 miles to the west and would not have been much help anyway. The following day she was forced to report to Sable Island station and confirm that she did not carrying any survivors of *Titanic* after rumours that Colonel John Jacob Astor was on board, a special train awaiting him when the ship arrived in Halifax. Such specific information shows how stories can emerge based on very little when people are clinging to hope.

Parisian continued her life at sea until being sold for scrap in 1914 and being sent over to Italy to be broken up.

29

Antillian

Type	Liner
Length	420.9 feet
Gross tonnage	5,613
Built	Caird & Co., Greenock
Owners	Leyland Line
Link to *Titanic* story	Received ice reports in vicinity of *Titanic*

The single-screw steamer *Antillian* started life on 20 September 1898 when she was launched from her Scottish building yard. She made her first voyage from Greenock to New Orleans on 9 December that same year, arriving at her destination on 27 December, so not a very fast ship but competent in her role. In 1901, her new owners were F. Leyland & Co. Ltd, also known as the Leyland Line, and she began service with them on New Year's Day on the transatlantic general routes to both North and South American ports.

Antillian was in the Mid-Atlantic heading eastbound on 14 April 1912 when she received an ice report from the fellow Leyland liner *Californian* at 1930 hours giving the position

Antillian. (*Titanic* Inquiry Project)

of the ice as 42.3N 49.9W. This was acknowledged by the ship and is known to have been heard by *Titanic* because the operator messaged back 'It's all right I've heard you sending to the *Antillian*.'

Just over a month later, on 30 May 1912, *Antillian* was on a voyage from Liverpool to Tampico when she ran onto a reef just off Turk's Island in the Caribbean. Despite all efforts to free the ship, the liner remained stuck, and the crew began to evacuate the passengers and mail, which was done with much difficulty according to the details provided in later press reports. The damage she had sustained was significant with flooding in Nos 1, 2 and 4 holds, the latter with up to 6 feet of water, and the rough sea making salvage operations almost impossible.

Several days later the ship was still on the reef and taking on even more water. No. 1 hold now had 14 feet and Nos 2 and 3 holds 8 feet, although the boiler and engine rooms were kept clear of any water by the continuous operation of the pumps and the huge efforts of her dedicated crew down below. Her cargo was taken off and transported to shore, the ship having now been stuck on the reef for over a month. There were continual attempts to salvage her, but nothing seemed to move *Antillian* from the reef. It was not until 2 July that she was finally pulled free and could be taken into port to be inspected. The shipping reports in the press stated that the hull of the ship was uninsured. Needless to say, the owners probably breathed a sigh of relief at this point.

Antillian continued to serve her transatlantic routes for many more years to come, her time sat on the reef seemingly having no detrimental effect on her. The remainder of her career was uneventful and she was eventually sold for scrap and broken up at Barrow in Lancashire in 1930.

30

Asian

Type	Liner
Length	420.6 feet
Gross tonnage	5,613
Built	Caird & Co., Greenock
Owners	Leyland Line
Link to *Titanic* story	In contact with *Titanic* and rescue ships

The screw steamer *Asian* was very much like the *Antillian*, having the same owners and builders, and was launched on 4 August 1898 as the *Columbian*. She was a black-hulled passenger and cargo vessel with a single funnel and two masts. She could carry only a few dozen passengers (just thirty-eight in First Class) but her role had significantly changed by 5 November 1899 when she became 'Boer War Transport Number 39'. She spent twenty-eight days transporting the 10th Royal Hussars to South Africa, on one occasion taking over the transporting of B Squadron when another ship, *Ismore*, was wrecked in St Helena Bay, 100 miles north of Cape Town. *Columbian* and three lighters were there to render assistance as the troops safely made it to the nearby shore.

On New Year's Day 1900, the ship was officially taken over by the Leyland Line and renamed *Asian*. She would now make trips to and from the US, slowly trudging back and forth carrying cargo and her few passengers.

On the early morning of Monday 15 April 1912, *Asian* was sailing westbound, towing an oil tank steamer called *Deutschland* 300 miles away from the sinking *Titanic*. *Deutschland* had run out of coal earlier and had required a tow on its voyage from Stettin to Philadelphia. That morning *Asian* picked up the distress calls from *Titanic* but was unable to attend, although she did relay the calls to other ships and was one of only two ships (*Virginian* being the other) that heard the final transmission at 0217 hours, 'two faintly sounding Vs', and then nothing. Therefore, she carried on to Halifax with the tanker in tow. This may be how the rumour that *Titanic* was being towed to Halifax started or was misheard in radio transmissions, but it is impossible to say for sure. *Asian* and *Deutschland* arrived safely in Halifax on 18 April.

During the First World War, *Asian* was attacked by a U-boat in the English Channel but incredibly the torpedo missed, and the ship was saved. However, her luck ran out on the early morning of 17 September 1924 when, on a voyage from New Orleans to Liverpool with a general cargo, during a severe gale she grounded on Stag Rocks, near the Old Head of Kinsale, Ireland (where *Lusitania* had been sunk nine years previously).

As the ship was pounded by waves and the wind, the radio operator managed to send out just one distress call before the mast collapsed and fell. Thankfully, nearby vessels heard it

Asian. (Unknown)

and raced to the scene, including the Dutch tug *Witte Zee* and the S-Class destroyer HMS *Seawolf*, the latter having been at anchor at Castletown until hearing the distress call. The six-year-old warship, built in Scotland and 276 feet long, sported a number of medium-sized guns on her upper decks but her 27,000 SHP turbines could push her at an impressive 36 knots, very helpful in a rescue operation where speed was of the essence. Meanwhile, on board *Asian* were seventy-five crew and six passengers, two of these children. As the ship was being evacuated a lifeboat upturned, killing one of the crew members, fireman Patrick Flood.

The terrified and stricken survivors of the boat were in the water for around half an hour before they were picked up by another lifeboat. After three hours, *Seawolf* arrived on the scene and finding the liner abandoned, attention was turned to searching for the lifeboats that had already been drifting for two hours in the severe storm. *Seawolf* successfully brought all personnel on board and landed them at the port of Bantry, a sailing time of around ten hours for them. Those on board the warship said that the passengers behaved 'splendidly'. It very soon became apparent that *Asian* was lost. With her insurance only £35,000, a small figure for a ship of this size, her loss would be a huge blow for the Leyland company. Within twenty-four hours the ship had broken in two just forward of her No. 2 hatch.

A day after their ordeal, forty-nine survivors were landed at Liverpool from Holyhead. Chief Officer P. Walton described one of the children, a seven-year-old boy, who had been listening to stories of pirates during the voyage and on seeing HMS *Seawolf* during the rescue cried out, 'Are those the pirates?' Needless to say, his mind was put at rest.

Today, the wreck lies in 18 metres of water and has been explored by divers many times over the last hundred years. Although it is very broken up, with wreckage spread over a wide area, parts of the engines and prop shaft can still be seen on the seabed.

Bibliography and Sources

Books

Ballard, Robert D., *The Discovery of the Titanic*
Delaunoy, Philippe, *SS Nomadic: Titanic's Little Sister*
Harrison, Leslie, *A Titanic Myth: The Californian Incident*
Marcus, Geoffrey, *The Maiden Voyage*

Websites

Encyclopaedia Titanica
Historic Ships Network
PaulLee.com
TitanicInquiry.org
Online newspaper archives for *Daily Mail, Daily Telegraph, The Times, Daily Mirror, Daily Express* and *Guardian*

Acknowledgements

I would like to thank all the people who have talked to me about *Titanic* over the last three decades. On acquiring a gift voucher for Waterstones book shop many years ago, I bought a collection of accounts of the remarkable story of *Titanic*. This has led me to many great things, including book writing, public speaking and, most of all, a career at sea lasting over twenty years.

The one person who I would like to say a big thank you to is my wife, Juliette. Her love and support throughout my research have meant that sometimes we just talked *Titanic* for hours while I worked on my writing and data-hunting.

Trevor Baxter, for chatting to me about the lost graves of *Titanic*. He directed me to the grave of Captain Haddock of the *Olympic* which was not far from where I was living. Chris Wardlow, the only other *Titanic* enthusiast near me when I was a kid. To all those who now regularly chat to me about the ship that launched my career in writing and who still keep in contact with me today.

Finally, I would like to thank all those who support me by sharing my social media posts, buying my books and attending events when I give a talk or when I unveil a new memorial plaque. Without all these people my work would not be worth doing.

Also by Richard M. Jones

The Great Gale of 1871
Lockington: Crash at the Crossing
Capsized in the Solent: The SRN6-012 Disaster
End of the Line: The Moorgate Disaster
Collision in the Night: The Sinking of HMS Duchess
Royal Victoria Rooms: The Rise and Fall of a Bridlington Landmark
RMS Titanic: The Bridlington Connections
The 50 Greatest Shipwrecks
Britain's Lost Tragedies Uncovered
The Burton Agnes Disaster
When Tankers Collide: The Pacific Glory Disaster
The Diary of a Royal Marine: The Life and Times of George Cutcher
The Farsley Murders
Living the Dream, Serving the Queen
Boleyn Gold (fiction)
Austen Secret (fiction)
Gunpowder Wreck (fiction)
Around the World in Shipwreck Adventures
Cretil the Cat (children's book)
Lost at Sea in Mysterious Circumstances
A–Z of Bridlington
Shipwrecks of the Solent
The Forgotten Submarine Pioneers
A–Z of Scarborough
Yorkshire Railway Disasters
Titanic: The Searches and the Dives